DATE DUE

ANTI-NATION:
Transition to Sustainability

ANTI-NATION:
Transition to Sustainability

FRED KNELMAN

◹ Mosaic Press
"Publishers for Canadian Communities"

CANADIAN CATALOGUING IN PUBLICATION DATA

Knelman, Fred H., 1919-
   Anti-nation
ISBN 0-88962-094-6 bd. ISBN 0-88962-093-8 pa.
1. Environmental policy — Canada. 2. Conservation
of natural resources — Canada. 3. Canada —
Economic policy. I. Title.
HC120.E5K54   301.31′0971   C78-001580-0

Published by Mosaic Press/Valley Editions, Box 1032, Oakville,
Ontario, L6J E59.

Published with the assistance of the Ontario Arts Council and
the Canada Council.

Printed in Canada on Canadian paper.
   •
ISBN 0-88962-094-6 cloth
      0-88962-095-8 paper

I wish to acknowledge the valuable assistance of
Suzy Gordon in the completion of this book.

Contents

Prologue

THIS BOOK HAS ITS ORIGIN in three stages of the author's intellectual development. Between 1950 and 1967 his ideas on modern technology were ripening. To a large degree the focus within this field was on nuclear technology. By 1970 a book was published by Wadsworth, "1984 and All That", embracing a new synthesis on the nature of modern technology. The major influence on the book was Jacques Ellul — as much a challenge for refutation as affirmation. Between 1967 and 1973 the environment tended to be the author's major concern, culminating in the experience of Dai Dong at the 1972 U.N. Conference on the Human Environment. (A paper on the author's contribution was published in Technology and Society Vol. 7 No. 4, November 1972 (pp. 112-117). A second paper, "The View from Stockholm" was published in International Affairs, October 1972 and analyzed global conflicts. By 1973 the author's interests had moved to a third stage, and a book was completed but never published; variously titled "Towards a Fourth World", "The Growth of Limits" and "Under No Flags". An essay version of this book was seen by Mosaic Press who were kind enough to commission this book in response.

The sense of the anachronism of sovereignty was a constant theme beginning almost with childhood. It was given specific form in an article, "Anti-Nation and Canadian Identity in the Nuclear Age", published in the Canadian journal Dimension, Vol. 4, No. 4, May-June 1967 (pp. 20-22). Between 1970 and the present, energy began to share concern with environment not as a replacement but as a search for unity in policy and program. One result was the writing of "Energy Conservation", Back-

13

ground Study No. 33, Science Council of Canada. Independently the exploration for societies organized to serve equity and environment and derived from ecological principles became of fundamental interest. It was fortunate to have been attached to the Science Council of Canada in 1973 and to have participated in the conceptualization of the Conserver Society study. A special aspect of the energy problem, namely nuclear power, resulted in the book "Nuclear Energy: The Unforgiving Technology" in late 1976 although the book also experimented with various previous streams of intellectual and political concern. The book was a command performance, written in three months under pressure but nevertheless a valuable exercising of ideas.

This book will be largely a conceptual voyage across the most turbulent areas of the current global debate. We will begin by identifying problems, global and national. We will select those problems which we feel are most urgent, i.e. most threatening to the world and to Canada. This selection will include an analysis of our Canadian social system and its problems. It is to these national problems we must assign the priority for seeking solutions. In the following section we will pick up major themes in the global debate. We have chosen two of these as exceedingly critical, questions of growth and the nature of contemporary technology.

At this stage in our book we will embark on a historical review of responses and attitudes to the environment, concentrating on a few basic concepts which are most significant to the ultimate propositions. The notion of a sustainable society and the nature of conservation are prominent among these concepts. Also included will be some thoughts on future studies.

We will next attempt to apply our conceptual schemes to the specific conditions of Canada. This will require an elucidation of the relevant history and present political economy of Canada.

Finally we will propose a radically new system for the future and will attempt to describe it in broad terms. Critical to this aspect of our book and to its entire development will be the analysis of the political economy of transition.

In illuminating our picture of a future Canada we will return to relate its patterns to the solution of our most urgent problems and hopefully the resolution of major conceptual ideological and philosophical conflicts. Thus the circle will close with a return to the beginning.

Anti-nation is the title of this book because it seems an essential ingredient of the new society we will discuss. Anti-nation is analagous to anti-matter. It is not non-nationhood but rather a nation which has radically transformed the norms of nationhood in order that the political economy more closely

14

matches ecological systems. Canada has a special problem and challenge in that it is, at least in content, multi-national. It is also extremely diverse — geographically, geopolitically, demographically etc. In effect Canadian conflicts mirror global conflicts and if solutions and resolutions can be discovered here we will have provided a model for the survival of the planet.

This book will break with academic tradition partially because of limitations of time but also because of inclination of spirit. Readers are cautioned at the outset not to expect neat formulae for the solution of problems or the resolution of conflicts. The book is an invitation to share the search. At best it may offer the potential paths, the occasional signposts and some travel guides for necessary change. We will not use reference notes nor provide mammoth bibliographies. Only a limited number of thinkers and their works have provided the major stimuli for the ideas expressed in this book. Some of these are recent. Others date back to the early beginnings of the search for comprehensiveness and cohesion. Reference will be made to them throughout the book. However, special acknowledgements are due to Ivan Illich, Hazel Henderson, Amory Lovins, Gordon Rattray Taylor, E.F. Schumacher, Kenneth Boulding, Jacques Ellul, G. West Churchman, Thomas Mann, Karl Marx, Pierre Dansereau, James Robertson, Simone de Beauvoir, Erich Fromm, Herbert Marcuse, Lewis Mumford, Thomas Kuhn and R.D. Laing. In the special cases where we are dealing with specifics of either numbers or words we will identify the source in the text and only by author. At the back of the book we will present by subject or theme the complete list of books from which these specifics have been drawn.

It is difficult to trace authorship of the phrase "the sustainable society." Dennis Clark Pirages edited a reader published in 1977 titled *The Sustainable Society* without assigning parenthood to the phrase. The major distinction between Pirages' book and this one is that Pirages focusses on the concept of sustainable growth which this author rejects as a non-resolvable duality. "Sustainable growth" is a contradiction in terms and concepts. The "law of minimum" limits sustainable growth unless one adopts a theory of infinite substitutions, ie. technical fixes forever. Sustainability is only possible in the long run at no growth or even negative growth.

While the concept of sustainability is not new, the actual term "the sustainable society" first came to this author's attention when used by a member of New Zealand's Values Party in Aukland.

The emerging consensus on sustainability is a form of cultural evolution whereby small social changes, ie. more highly evolved sub-systems or groups, become a precursor for a new society.

The concepts and conceptual schemes dealt with in this book are universal, independent of nation, region or level of development. The actual case chosen for illustration, Canada, is in part due to the unique set of social, political, cultural and geo-political conditions that pertain to Canada and secondly due to the author's familiarity and familiality with the Canadian scene. The sum of these allowed a higher level of visualizing and even operationalizing the transition to a sustainable society.

Chapter 1

The New Agenda

The Nature of Our Times

ALL REVOLUTIONS BEGIN in time and space within impossible
conditions for success. At the beginning of all great periods of
change the forces resisting change out-weigh those promoting
it. The historical perspective, nevertheless, tells us that revolutions succeed no matter how small their beginnings. Viable ideas
that are part of necessary history are irresistible and, like energy,
cannot be destroyed. It seems a characteristic of all great social
revolutions that they develop from streams of convergence or
lines of resonance where small effects multiply, converge and
resonate until a great qualitative change results and a new wave
is created. The conditions for necessary change now exist and
are ripe, seeking the means of their fulfillment.

As yet there is no agreement on the means for averting
disasters or measuring their rate of approach or assigning
priorities for action. For some, disaster will be upon us sooner
than later and revolution not reform is the answer. These
differences must be studied to weigh their relative merit. But to
begin with, it is a particular, emerging consensus we must
examine and describe.

This growing consensus of concern, this "revolution of
hope", is a world-wide phenomenon, crossing all political
geographical and ideological boundaries. This must come to
represent the new politics of survival and the basis of what Ellul
calls the "necessary revolution". But problems of definition,
communication, information and validation can confuse the
main concern, deliberately or innocently.

A fundamental question is whether the "revolution of hope"
is realistic or simply an idle or pious fantasy. Are we condemned

17

to the "perpetual cycle of failure" sprinkled occasionally with brave attempts? Even Aurobindo's concept is unreal in that a few more failures or even the major failure of nuclear war will remove all perpetuity. The world could end either through "a bang or a whimper". The more lilely scenarios of the future are breakthroughs through breakdowns. We will likely end up in a form of the sustainable society but by default and at great cost of leaps of discontinuity. We must choose the path of opportunity and crisis avoidance if our sustainable society is to be one of grace.

The world is witnessing a universal crisis manifested by profound disorder and unrest and other, more subtle symptoms of social disease. It is the view of this author that while this crisis resides externally in the economic, political and cultural institutions and structures of various societies, it also lies in the human heart and mind. We are not speaking here of psychological disorders (although these are symptoms) but the critical choices that determine our future. Until enough people share this view, meaningful change will not occur. We require a general understanding that the future is no longer assured without active human intervention to ensure it.

Above all this is an age of multiple crises of human value and belief systems, those operational sets of choices and priorities which represent the observed decisions of our lives and the life of nations and societies. We must come to this conclusion because the crisis is universal and largely independent of ideology, philosophy or theology. What we now call the energy crisis or the new economic crisis are only early warnings. This is not to deny the dynamic interchange between society and human values. Nor does it suggest we must await a profound psychosocial revolution before we can solve the basic problems of society. In fact we are urging the reverse. We change ourselves in the act of changing the world.

The survival crisis, itself, is a symptom and we must ask ourselves what are the underlying causes?

The history of the world exhibited a major discontinuity about 1970 which was not reflected in the consciousness of the majority or the decisions of the powerful — tragic omissions in both cases. A new future was suddenly upon us and the number of actors and interactions concerning the future exploded. By the end of 1973 the global jolt was felt throughout the economically developed world.

The seventies may turn out to be the most prophetic time in the history of humankind. We are entering a period of critical change of global significance. The exponential horizon is curving downward into sygmoid reality. The thematic development of

18

this book will be to identify the nature of this change — really a paradigm shift from a world view based on unlimited growth to a new vision of equilibrium societies. Such changes are revolutionary in the broadest sense, infusing themselves into semantic as well as political environments.

Thomas Kuhn in his great work *The Structure of Scientific Revolutions* used the term "dominant paradigm" to signify entire sets of unquestioned assumptions, perceptions and ways of thinking about reality. It not only imposes a world view on society and all who share it but excludes certain questions or anomalies as meaningless. It tends to influence a total culture. The "industrial growth — progress — high technology" dominant paradigm is now beset by anomalies, dilemmas, paradoxes and contradictions which it can no longer ignore or cast off. These multiple and irreconcilable dilemmas are intensified by the new scarcity hitting a society based on the assumption of endless plenty. And, perhaps, more importantly, a new plenty of environmental degradation has inflicted a deep wound on the system. The world is ripe for a paradigm shift, a new vision which resolves these anomalies.

We require a serious reorientation of some of our major goals, internally and externally. In some ways we need inversions of normal nationalistic policy. The key to such a national program is the fusing of two visions, so often in conflict. These may be represented by the ecological imperative and the politics of equity. Hopefully a unified vision will lead to planetary unity.

The second half of the sixties witnessed an unprecedented rise in the visibility of pollution in economically developed countries. This environmental deterioration seemed unrelated to socio-economic systems. The U.S.A., the U.S.S.R., Canada and Sweden all experienced ominous symptoms. Unprecedented economic growth was increasingly acknowledged as generating excessive environmental costs. Most major urban centres and concentrated industrialized regions were cloaked in a permanent pall of air pollution. Dramatic deterioration in environmental quality occurred within an unexpectedly short time. Almost daily, new polluting sources and symptoms were being identified. It was finally realized that even global ecosystems were vulnerable.

This rising visibility of environmental degradation and the multiplicity of threats triggered a vast increase in public concern. Environmental groups emerged throughout the economically developed world. In almost every country such groups, together with environmental scientists, activated a new perception in which unbridled industrialization and urbanization were identified as major sources of the problem. At the same time, governments became actively involved as a result of their own recognition of the problem and through external pressures. By the end of the decade, it was realized that the threat was indeed global, critical and unacceptable. Hans J. Morgenthau was quoted in Newsweek (March 18, 1974, p. 6) — "The nation-state is now too small an entity to protect the life, liberty and happiness of its own citizens." This globalization of problems is now both a threat and a promise.

The Quadrilemma — Four of the Most Urgent Problems in the World
TODAY WE CAN IDENTIFY some of those problems whose scope and urgency threaten the survival of civilization. To some degree we can even quantify the path of their development but as yet cannot predict accurately the timing of disaster. There are four most urgent problems in the world; but as we do not as yet have solutions they remain dilemmas — energy / resources, equity / distribution, environment and population with its special aspect of urbanization. These are not unrelated, but intimately connected. They all represent "Malthusian" dilemmas lodged in uncontrolled and unlimited growth. Due to the lag of the necessary mechanisms of social control, both as institutions and belief systems, these dilemmas will inevitably lead to disaster. They are the "bombs" (P. Ehrlich), "crashes" (G. Rattray Taylor) and "traps" (K. Boulding) leading to population explosions, ecological Armageddon, energy and resource wars or wars of redistribution as the have-nots fight for their share of survival. And the ultimate threat is that war becomes nuclear war. Maldistribution of consumption means maldistribution of health, wealth and justice. It exists within nations and between nations. The new communications have created the "global village" of McLuhan in the sense of instant distribution of information and rising expectancies. But expectancy has risen much faster than fulfillment and the reality of the maldistribution of consumption between economically developed nations and the developing world is such that the vast majority of people in the world can never consume at the U.S.'s or Japan's present level. They can never even catch up. Increasing the current tensions is the fact that resources are not distributed in the earth's crust in accordance to the distribution of economic power, the cases of oil and uranium being most prominent.

The growing maldistribution of consumption between the have and the have-not nations of the world is critically divisive. It was the pivotal issue at the UN Conference on the Human Environment in June 1972 and the UN conferences on food, population, habitat and the seas that followed. When it is understood that each American in their lifetime consumes about 40 times the energy and most major resources of that of a person in the Third World and that each Canadian consumes perhaps 30 times and that these countries continue on their manifest destiny of high exponential growth, one then realizes that it is not possible for the Third World to ever catch up and one must accept that this maldistribution dilemma cannot be resolved except by drastic revolutionary re-distribution systems. Together Canada and the U.S.A. with about 245 million people are equivalent to 10 billion Third Worlders in their consumption. It should be noted that this maldistribution dilemma is also characteristic of group disparities within nations. Unlimited growth is impossible for any biological species. But we have extended the concept of limits of growth to include environmental degradation and urbanization. It is true that the uncontrolled proliferation of nuclear power — civil and military — constitutes the major military threat for global destruction. For the purposes of this book we are absorbing nuclear issues within the energy problems. These are all types of "Malthusian" dilemmas. In this sense military nuclear technology is definitely such a dilemma, growing at rates significantly higher than the control systems' — world law and order, international mediation, etc. — which would or could prevent its ultimate use.

The essential meaning of "Malthusian dilemmas" is that a real limit always exists to the growth of any population of a particular species within a habitat having ultimately finite resources of matter and energy. We have merely identified four such dilemmas as representing the most urgent problems that confront the world and threaten survival. We have called this group of four most urgent problems — The Quadrilemma — after Dennis Gabor, Nobel Laureate, who, in his book, "Inventing the Future," used the term "trilemma." We have also extended the concept of a "Malthusian" dilemma to areas other than human populations. We may also extend this concept of population limits to technology and the same analogy may be applied to automobile, aeroplane or weapons' populations. In each case with continued growth, a point of stress is inevitably reached, either through space, energy, resource depletion or the lag of controls, i.e. the general growing disparity between population or traffic in biological and technological systems and the controls necessary to moderate, mediate and direct these populations. The great Western Energy crises are the first major manifestation of limits, although these are largely political and geopolitical. In the same way another dilemma in our quadrilemma is the problem of the global maldistribution of consumption between the economically developed and developing world.

44940

Here the dilemma is the difference in consumption rates and quantities and without a major redistribution coupled with a slowing down or levelling off in consumption in the economically developed world this dilemma is leading to global disaster.

The population dilemma is multi-faceted. Its broadest face is the maldistribution of resources, particularly food, with its increasing stress of under-nutrition and malnutrition among the poor, highly populated regions of the world. Population is itself maldistributed so that increasing numbers live in large urban centres incapable of providing adequate life support systems, plagued by cancerous growth and facing unsurmountable social and environmental costs.

When we use the concept "Malthusian dilemma" we are also pointing to an existing "cultural lag", for example a lag between traffic and controls or population and life-support systems. We have proposed a term for the world's four most urgent problems i.e. the "quadrilemma", each of which constitutes in itself a "Malthusian dilemma." These problems are not distinct but linked in a complex web and we are not purporting to solve them in isolation from each other, although priorities for solution can shift in time and space. Crises avoidance technologies can be as significant as opportunity technologies. Emergency response technologies may be equally significant for critical developments.

Actually the "Malthusian dilemma" is not just a problem of the select sub-systems described but one of the entire system. The systemic problem is one of complexity outgrowing control, noise outgrowing communication and disorder drowning order. This is the "macroproblem".

It should be made clear that these are not the only problems but seemingly the most urgent global problems. Other problems such as nationalism, agriculture, water, employment, etc. are extremely significant as well. Moreover all problems mentioned are both global and national i.e. they are problems of the world but also of Canada. It will be our purpose to propose national approaches to solutions which will have global applicaton, connection or significance. We will also not ignore the secondary problems. But it is our belief that these, to a very large degree, are derivative and internal, although, of course, not entirely. It will be partly our task to weave the web of their inter-relationships. We have, as mentioned, deliberately chosen not to deal with the problem of war, particularly because we believe it is the problem of problems. Satisfactory resolutions of energy, equity and environment problems will tend to remove the causes of war.

We have identified four basic global social dilemmas. These

are: (1) Equity or Maldistribution; (2) Environment; (3) Energy/ Resources; and (4) Population/Urbanization. We shall not give these equal weight in treatment in part due to their complexity and to questions of their relative urgency and primacy. Rather we shall seek our focus within the real global agenda dominated as it has been by the issues of energy, growth, development, equity and technology. We shall put considerable emphasis on the questions of nuclear power, civil and military, since it involves both energy and technology. Also Canada as a particular form of federal state, while not unique, presents certain problems which are critical to our analysis. These will require special attention aside from the great global issues. It will be our hope to relate national and international solutions as a unified program.

Chapter 2

The Great Global Debates

THE BEST WAY to describe the global agenda is to focus on the content of current global debates. These generally correspond to the "quadrilemma" which we have previously discussed. They are Environment, Energy, Equity and Economics — the fours E's. The economics issue has two major aspects — growth and technology, the traditional vehicle of growth. Attached to these are a cluster of purely economic problems, i.e. employment, inflation, trade balances, monetary issues, trade and aid. But behind and beyond this there is a fundamental purpose to provide society with those goods and services which assure survival, allow fulfillment and have long-term sustainability. Energy is the fundamental force or the tool which lies behind all the goods and services which we need or desire. The energy system is a special case of technology. Environment comprises Nature's gift of essential environmental goods and services as well as the physical, biological and built environments in which we live, produce, consume and waste. While we require energy to provide the basic needs for living and surviving, the environment is both a gift and a constraint. We must protect the gift but live within our environmental means, that is we must live within limits. Equity is the ultimate historical human value which affirms that all people are created equal, have inalienable rights, should be provided with the opportunities for realizing rights and self-realization. It is the driving force of political action within and between nations.

The agenda of the special UN sessions since 1972 tend to conform to our "quadrilemma" although the Four E's tend to underlie both national and international debates. The E's are often posited as dualistic when taken any two at a time. These so-called dualities such as Energy/Environment, Economics/Energy, Economics/Equity, Economics/Environment etc. are sometimes real, often apparent and manipulated. Not only must we attempt to resolve all dualities, real or apparent, but we must recognize that such an ultimate resolution deals with entire complex systems. A major problem as we have suggested is that the system is blind.

In this book we will tend to emphasize the four E's rather than the problems of "Malthusian dilemmas" or "cultural lags" which predates it by several decades. Under economics we shall concentrate on the growth debate, the debate about technology and the nature of development. In particular we believe contemporary economic theory is moribund.

The traditional world view is that continued growth is necessary to fulfill all human goals. A bigger pie is thought to be the answer to equity. A smaller pie is thought to be the answer to environment. The simplistic assumption is that of a direct linear relationship between GNP and energy consumption or GNP and technology. Resolution could come from emphasizing growth in quality, i.e. by enhancing nutritional value or by making many small pies each maximizing quality. Nevertheless, the demands of population and consumption on the size of the pie will be profound. The depletion/pollution impacts will be equally powerful. And the demand for an equitable division of goods and services will go on unabated and perhaps indifferent to constraints or opportunities alike.

Of all the debates the one concerning growth and viability of societies based on continued growth has become globalized and dominant since 1972. The Club of Rome's three sponsored studies, "The Limits to Growth", "Mankind At the Turning Point" and "RIO — Restoring the International Order" have done much to stimulate the debate but neither really dealt with alternatives. At the same time it is not possible to debate the growth question without dealing with the nature of contemporary technology. While each has its own intellectual and social history they are interdependent and most often intrinsically linked. In this chapter we shall deal with these two major global debates.

To Grow or Not to Grow
ECONOMIC GROWTH AS the dominant orientation of policy in almost all societies independent of their stage of economic development or the ideological base of the state is perhaps the fundamental debate of our time. Big government and big business have put its money where its mouth is, i.e. in the

planning of bigger, better and more powerful technologies, military and civil. The major resources of our society are allocated to "business as usual" programs supported by the "conventional wisdom of our times."

The debate on growth was publicly launched with the release of the Club of Rome's sponsored study "The Limits to Growth". It very quickly became apparent that there would be "no limit to the growth debate". But despite the proliferation of words the serious content of the debate was sewn into the future and a new dialogue began to emerge.

Thus in spite of the deterioration of the limits to growth debate to a methodological tournament in which Lockean and Leibnizian inquirers became locked into a debate of multiple monologues, the Forrester model applied by Meadows has a message beyond methodology. This is the universal ecological principle of ultimate limits to all growth. Also the more critical defects of the Meadows study such as the use of aggregated data, which disguised international, national and regional disparities and the neglect of the nuclear threat have been largely corrected in the Mesarovic study.

An interesting aspect of the "Limits to Growth" debate was what this author has terms the strange bedfellows response. Growth advocates and technocrats of the left and right combined to indict it with a broad array of sins of omission and commission. Without a blush of shame the modellers of the American economy and the war in Viet Nam joined in the attack on Forrester's methodology. The strange bedfellows response has been observed in the global population debate as well.

The Growth-Progress paradigm, riding on the back of unbridled technology, may be coming to an end. Its mythology is slowly succumbing to reality. The concept of unlimited growth is dying in the face of real depletion. The ideology of progress is being challenged by the ecological concept of the "stable or steady state". The myth that growth is the exclusive means to equity was never true. Now it is a shady irony when the pie is shrinking and the share of the poor is eroded by inflation. The magic numbers of growth, GNP and energy consumption per capita are increasingly questionable measures of social value. Profiligacy may well be the cause not the effect. To equate growth to development is to equate it to cancer.

The euphoria of the late sixties with its vision of unlimited growth has been shaken. The ecological impasse has been reinforced in the new found power of the powerless. Commodity clout is a dress rehearsal for living with permanent shortages, a global future shock. The system is being identified as the disease. Now the end of the oil age is in view on the exponential horizon. And in the telescoping of time through accelerated depletion, the world faces a continuous crunch of increasing pressure for at least the next three decades. The politics and economics of oil may well produce some of the most intense strains on the present precarious balance of power. And the Green Revolution which is thought of as the salvation for global hunger is a voracious consumer of petroleum and petroleum products. The ecological perspective is frightening. Food and fibre connect all humanity.

As expressed earlier it is the belief of this author that a "paradigm shift" or new world view of development is emerging expressed by the concepts of the stable-state, "steady-state" and "conserver society" or the term favoured, the sustainable society. The empirical and experiential failure of present growth societies is leading to a new convergence of intellectual and social forces around the need for "appropriate development". An integral part of this is appropriate, soft and intermediate technology.

The major confrontations of today are increasingly between economists and ecologists. Professor Conrad A. Istock of Rochester University has a neat fable to illustrate this: "Economics, Queen of the social sciences, became the Queen by marrying King Government. Thereby she initiated the family lineage of Political Economy, and the dominion of the royal family increased seemingly without bound. Now, after a long and seldom challenged reign, there are increasing rumours of discontent, even within that very private royal family itself. The unease is caused in large part by that errant Knight Ecology and his report of great troubles untended throughout the whole of the Kingdom..." We must affirm that it is virtually impossible to separate economics and politics. This is particularly so given our earlier social analysis of economically developed systems whereby politics as one of the major sub-systems is locked into the economic imperatives. Thus governments do not govern but adopt postures for re-election. Corporations in the act of "doing their thing" attempt to maximize returns on their invested capital by any means available. Adam Smith provided the original rationalization in 1776: "It is not the actual greatness of national wealth but its continual increase which occasions a rise in the wages of labour." This has been, from that time forward, the major rationale of the apostles of growth, whether traditional economists or corporate and government heads. A larger GNP has been supposed to lead both to greater social benefits and to a superior distribution of these benefits. That there is a threshold below which a perfectly equitable system could not provide the basic necessities for every citizen is true, but that growth has automatically created greater equitability or even that it is genuine growth is highly questionable. The proportion of poor remains about constant in the U.S.A. and Canada. Meanwhile increased uncontrolled growth has brought with it an exponential rise in social costs, i.e. in the disbenefits and diseconomies arising from the side effects. In a parody of the real issue, growth maniacs confront ecofreaks. But the game of growth is tragic. Someone paraphrased the tragedy as a parallel to the laws of thermodynamics: (1) We can't win; (2) We are sure to lose; and, (3) There is no other game."

What Edmund Burke called the "sophisters, economists and calculators" have not been able to calculate the human factor and in their blind advocacy of growth have helped to create the great moral crisis of our times. Economists like behaviorists have attempted, in mechanistic fervour, to reduce the human equation to a profit-loss balance sheet, quantified by the exclusive currency of the realm-money-within a mystique of the "invisible hand of the free" market. Yet there is as yet no arithmetic of human welfare.

For the first time in modern history — at least since Adam Smith — some economists are beginning to question their own dominant assumptions and methodologies. 'Post-Keynesian economics', dominated by the earlier work of John Maynard Keynes and the later work of Alfred Marshall, has led and directed the economic policies of the U.S.A. and the other Western industrialized states. The great power of the "post-Keynesian Synthesis", demonstrated by the phenomenal development in the post World War II period, attached a kind of godlike virtue to economic growth. This euphoria lasted to the 1950's when cracks in the system began to appear. Among the most prominent cracks were the increased visibility of the "invisible poor", the serious side effects arising from the concentration of power in the industrial-military complex and the accompanying military commitment, the conflict of priorities, the racial conflicts, the seesaw of inflation and employment, the international monetary crisis, the ideological and developmental division of the world, the energy crisis, continuing war and then the slow emergence of the huge burden of hidden social costs such as pollution, poverty etc. The world is still waiting for a John Maynard Keynes of the "steady-state", but an influential group of economists like Boulding, Mishan, Daly, Georgescu-Roegen, Ward and Galbraith have begun to attack the "post-Keynesian synthesis" and to search for a humane economics. Despite our criticism of Keynes, in the 1930's he did write a prophetic essay entitled "The Economic Possibilities for Our Grandchildren" which dealt with purposiveness. In part he wrote, "The 'purposive' man is always trying to secure a spurious and delusive immortality for his acts by pushing his interest in them forward into time. He does not love his cat, but his cat's kittens: nor, in truth, the kittens, but only the kitten's kittens, and so on forward forever to the end of cat-dom. For him jam is not jam unless it is a case of jam tomorrow and never jam today. Thus by pushing his jam always forward into the future, he strives to secure for his act of boiling it an immortality." Of course, the view from the dispossessed cannot have this future orientation and this is why we have stressed the maldistribution dilemma. The majority of peoples of the world still live with "Malthusian" dilemmas as their reality.

The Growth of Limits

IN PART, THE PROBLEM of those who support a blind faith in the power of technology to extend the limits of growth arises out of the natural system of inter-corporate, inter-regional and international competition, by its nature a violation of the ecological principle of indivisibility. Any solution operating at some level of the system less than the dimension of the whole system is doomed to failure. Jay W. Forrester of M.I.T. refers to the "counterintuitive behaviour of social systems" but this is a disagreeable term inasmuch as using a human quality to describe an institution is highly questionable. As a characteristic of social systems, it seems true but the word is also unacceptable. Counter-systemic and certainly counter-productive are more accurate terms. Since the largest operational system is the planet itself, any limited systems approaches are doomed to be anti-ecological. In terms of humans, the design capacity and of course the creative and imaginative capacity, exceeds the analytical capacity particularly in their ability to analyze a complex system of interacting factors. The work of the Club de Rome and the publications on the limits of growth should not be judged on the reliability of their predictions or even in their methods of quantifying factors and certainly not in all of their basic assumptions, but rather on the general principle they imply. We must all grow to accept these principles and such an acceptability is better described as the growth of limits because this concept does not attempt to be precise in its predictions.

The spectrum of responses that have been mobilized against the Meadows study may be grouped into clusters represented by methodological, ideological, technological and economic arguments. Methodological objections span the accusation that the model is the message or as Christopher Freeman put it the "Malthus in — Malthus out" bias to the Lockean arguments about the thin data base, the weakness of the assumed

THE GREAT GLOBAL DEBATES

relationships in the feedback loops and the non-probalistic nature of the predictive process. The technological critics noted the absence of salvation technology or a "technological optimist curve" which allows for the assumptions of continuous growth in efficiency, continuous substituion, the infinite resource base in the crust of the earth etc. The economic argument also resting on technological optimism insisted that market mechanisms controlled shortages and that the drift to a service economy and public rather than private goods would solve the problem of limited growth. Ideological attacks affirmed their faith that Malthus had always been wrong in the past, that the proper ideology could solve the problem and that to freeze growth was to freeze inequity. The question was posed. Who pays the cost of slow or no growth? At the same time they counterposed political violence and structural violence, the justice of formal legalities and distributive justice.

Nevertheless the experience of the real world suggests that the growth paradigm of imperatives by positive feedback using knowledge as power to triumph over Nature through the application of endless techniques is a sum-zero game. Planned waste is both disastrous and robs the future. The gross anomalies of inflation coupled with unemployment, social unrest, pollution and stress, war and famine finally cannot be served by a "grosser national product". The energy crisis of 1973-74, the winter of our discontent was a dress rehearsal of the future. The issue reduces itself to this. Convergence to low growth will occur either by the "invisible hand" or "invisible foot" with its increasing visibility as a fist or foot aimed at stability. Or we must move gracefully to sustainability by conscious planning to avoid costly discontinuities.

The political argument which affirms that in the real dis-aggregated world there are nations and regions which require growth is undeniable. This poses the dilemma of maldistribution and its apparent conflict with the ecological imperative. Must the rich become poorer for the poor to become richer? The question masks issues of values concerning the quality and quantity of life. There are countries in the world with half the energy consumption per capita of Canada and the U.S. and nevertheless a wide range of superior social indicators. In organizing the need to redistribute given the wide range of consumption levels in the world there are implicit limits to the expansion of consumption in the economically developed world. But economic growth or production growth can never in itself lead to distributive justice, whether it is growth peddled by the West or the new elitist affluence in the Third World.

There are other aspects to the concept of the growth of

limits that are important. These have to do with energy and communication. There is a thermodynamic law of entropy which in its simplest sense means that in every transformation of energy some of the exchanged energy is irrecoverable as output and is lost to the environment as heat. In a popular sense we call this thermal pollution and it is always associated with energy production. It imposes an ultimate limit on global energy consumption, the threat being unacceptable climate change. The time scale of this limit could be of the order of 50 years based on present energy growth projections.

Events have already imposed permanently lower growth rates on Western developed economics. Nevertheless there is no committed plan for an economics and politics of transition. Such a plan would probably incorporate a rate of growth sufficient to serve a reduced population rate of increase for a period of some 40 to 50 years of small but finite increase in population. The strategy of transition rests clearly on an approach to zero population growth and a "compression" economy, i.e. Oscar Morgenstern's concept of an economy serving the kernel of real needs and with all waste removed.

Trend is not Destiny

IT IS NOT POSSIBLE to settle the question of defining actual, i.e. operational, limits to growth without introducing assumptions which themselves reflect non-objective value judgements. Thus a "technological optimist" curve introduced into the Meadows model radically alters the output side of the analysis. Once technological fixes are assumed to be constant in time, i.e. constantly available in the future, then resources tend towards the infinite. Merely assuming that all the minerals in the earth's crust and oceans (also on the moon) will become available at an acceptable social cost and a payable price in the future pushes the limits upwards dramatically.

On the other hand, limits to waste pose a problem which while they cannot be simply quantified are nevertheless amenable to analysis which can provide some reasonable order of magnitude. The technological and/or growth euphoric would argue that limits to waste are equally amenable to fixes such as massive recycling and efficiency or waste shipments into space. However this requires radical institutional changes and in both the concept of unlimited growth or unlimited capacity to handle the wastes of growth, the real limits may well be the nature of social institutions and social capacities to control and regulate human activities on a regional, national and international scale.

William Ophuls and others have correctly defined this institutional adaptability limit in ecological terms, i.e. the "law of

31

the minimum". This means the factor which limits the growth of a complex dynamic system (see Forrester) is that which is least available. This factor is the capacity to manage human activities with the necessary asociated institutions so as to extend the optimum yield principle into all options. The situation is even worse in that we are steering society through the "rear view mirror" and on a cybernetic information scheme which is suffering from a lock-in malfunction, responding almost exclusively to positive feedback. The result is confusing the accelerator with the brake.

However a caution is necessary. It is not merely a transformation of managerial skills from the linear and hierarchal to the non-linear and participatory form that is lacking. Much more it is that the inventory of attitudes and institutions is locked into a redundant worldview. It is the political-economy of growth fed by an ideology of progress (left and right) dragging an adaptive culture that is the real obstacle to necessary change.

Sustainable Growth — The Ultimate Illusion

FOR THIS AUTHOR the concept of sustainable growth is self-contradictory. There are fewer and fewer growth addicts on the left and right who continue to support it. At some point in space and time sooner or later, societies will have to achieve a dynamic steady-state. Conceivably this would be multi-staged, i.e. sequential phases of S-curves moving upward or downwards but thresholds and ceilings would utlimately assert themselves through various forms of limiting or constraining factors which inhibit the exponential in the world as a whole or any other attainable worlds. It is of particular interest that growth advocates are still another case of the strange bedfellows phenomenon. The left and right advocate growth and castigate the "conserver" or "small is beautiful" and "limits to growth" groups as fascists, heretics or hippies. The left is concerned with equitable distribution and cannot conceive fulfillment except through growth. The right is concerned with expanding the spoils to meet their voracious appetites. Accountants who believe compound interest is sacred seem to be the guides for both groups. They also both eschew conventional paths of development a repeat of the history of industrialization but at accelerated rates with careless disregard for the absence of infrastructures. It is curious that the left supports equity through growth even when that growth is at the expense of equity. To support growth in the economically developed countries based as it is on the consumption of the global store of non-renewable resources is to deny the equitable distribution of these to the future world. Thus such a posture must rest on technological faith viz fusion or fission breeding or both. It is a closing circle in which the world turns out the same in both the visions of the left and the right and only the question of who rules that world remains critical. The withering away of the state becomes even more distant as the horizon is over-shadowed by the megastate and its megamachine.

It is true that there are advocates of "no growth" who are insensitive to the cause of equity. It is equally true that the dispossessed wish possessions as a priority over environmental concerns. Nations and people are more highly motivated by the desires of early equity than by concern for the more remote threats of environmental disruption. And yet the prospect of ¾ths of the world rushing through the industrial-urban process in a few decades to reach the levels of consumption and waste associated with economically developed countries is disastrous. Surely there is a better mode of development that provides the assurances of long-term survival combined with the capacity for fulfillment while avoiding the gross errors of threatening the environment. And surely that superior mode of development is easier to take earlier rather than later. The options are still open for most of the world and relatively closed for the economically developed countries. And surely it is incumbent on the rich and powerful countries to aid the less fortunate ones to equitability along a path that avoids as much of the costs of growth as possible.

There is a subtle underpinning to this debate among persons with common goals (excluding the deliberate exploiters and the psychotic fringe). To a large degree it has to do with world views or paradigms not least of which is perceptions of the power of science, technology.

Competing with the global debate on growth is the debate on technology. We have already discussed the profound gulf between technological optimists and pessimists. But we must proceed further analyzing the deeper nature of contemporary technology. The debate about technology is also a debate about energy and in particular nuclear energy. Actually as we have indicated it cannot be separated from the debate about growth.

Technology: Threat or Promise

THE SEMANTIC OR INTELLECTUAL environment has produced the ensemble of techniques (Ellul) or the sum of the technosphere and nomosphere (tools and techniques) i.e. Max Nicholson's or Robertson's technological imperative and institutional impera-tive. These have become the new social dynamics driving all the other elements of society. To a large degree each has become self-perpetuating and self-actuating, humans merely adapting and reinforcing blind goals as they become integrated into organizational roles within these various institutions. The pure Ellulian interpretation is a clear form of technological determinism viewing technology as the complete ensemble of techniques, of tools, tool-making and progams to modify and manipulate the physical, biological, psychological and social environment. It rests on a concept that "manipulative rationality" is omniscient.

At the outset we reject technological determinism as we reject the complete renunciation of technology. We believe there can be technology without tears as we believe we need technology to survive. But these attributes require a radical revision in the social relations of technology and in the social structure that must command it.

We also reject the polarization between technological optimism and pessimism. We note that proponents of soft technology often have a double standard indulging in soft technological fixes while eschewing the technological fix per se. We believe all technology must be directed by and for people.

A strange correspondence on this issue of technological optimism is that the economically developed world, communist and non-communist, share a common faith in science and technology, each side making this claim in the name of their own ideology or social system, that is given the "proper" socio-economic system then science and technology are automatically transformed into servants of the people and for human welfare, fulfillment. Thus the Russian and American new technocrats sound and speak alike. And even China makes these same claims at least with some positive evidence to support them. But it is the blind nature of the claim rather than the issue of possible Chinese "exceptionalism" that is being questioned here. It is yet uncertain what course China will take in the future, whether she will opt to move up in the hierarchy of power to superpower status, transforming science and technology into its "hard" and "big" forms and if so, whether she will produce the disbenefits and abuses associated with these developments in the other highly industrialized states. At present China is saying that these disbenefits and abuses are the result of the capitalist or revisionist socio-economic systems of the West and the U.S.S.R. Given the "proper" system, i.e. that of China, then technology will only produce social benefits.

It is true that all observers bring value judgements to bear not only on "trans-scientific" (Weinberg) questions but on "scientific" ones as well. And they often cloak their most cherished beliefs in "objectivity". At best, science as a social and human activity attempts to control its own limitations by stating them explicitly and by excluding questions which are by nature not amenable to its methodologies of investigation. Unfortunately science and scientists sometimes pose as the exclusive repositories of objectivity or even "truth" and this pose has been fed by their patrons in the large establishments of government, industry and university with the virtual sanctity of priesthood.

Science, Trans-Science and Anti-Science

THE QUESTION OF "objectivity" even the recognition of its relativeness relates to an even larger issue of the nature of science itself as a way of knowing and with its claims to "objectivity". The quotation marks are deliberate because this dispute is profound and would require a book in itself, not a minor diversion. Science is only one way of knowing and has its own built-in intrinsic limitations let alone the limits of the Pascal admonition "the heart has reasons which reason can never know." This is not to downgrade science as a way of knowing but to grade it with proper perspective. It is a single vision but a powerful one and not to be idly discarded.

Facts also, like objectivity are not really value-free, despite the assertion of the positivists who unfortunately cannot substantiate their own philosophy by its criteria of validation. Facts in themselves live in a situation in which there exists a pervasive social climate, an environment of values from which they cannot be totally abstracted. Scientism which is the religious and ideological form of science is the first theology to insist that it is not theological. It has many of the trappings of religion including its hierarchy of priests, its obscurantism, language, elitism, exclusivity, etc. And with this we have elitism and professionalism which excludes all non-members of the club of peers, measured by a formal set of credentials and productions. But science has been revealed as still another school of limited reality. We are also concerned about the new wave of anti-science rampant among a large section of youth and fed by certain contemporary works of both serious and spurious content and often blurred by faddists, cultists and other self-defeating and self-appointed high priests of the irrational. We must not succumb to "throwing away the baby with the bathwater" view of science. Admittedly the bath water is foul — the baby was scarred at birth, messed up and messy. Certainly the baby has contributed to fouling the water. But the abuse and misuse of science is not due to some mysterious, innate, psychologically and methodologically determined flaw of science and scientists, but through a social distortion and disorder. We should keep the baby after all, clean it up, gentle it down and

35

bring it up to be human. Arguments that the baby was so deformed and deranged at birth that euthanasia is prescribed are as unacceptable as assuming that science is the sole and exclusive voyage to the discovery of truth or reality. Rather the social use of science and technology was deformed and distorted by an early duality of function. It is true that science as a "sweet" and irresistible calling, a fruit both forbidden and bidden, is not different in its easthetics and creativity to poetry or painting. It is equally true that it has largely given way to a technocratizing process producing more over-specialized blinkered plodders operating in technical and social slots of the research and development bureau. The "sweetness" of science is now largely wasted in creating Strangelovian weapons of civil and military destruction and is overcome by the "euphoria of gadgetry". But this is not entirely true.

Pure science was never really pure except to purists but it is a legitimate, profound and necessary creativity of the human imagination, restricted yes, but no less than certain other ways of knowing. Its way still has immense social value if only in potentiality. We know orthodoxy smothers discovery in science as in other knowing and belief systems. But science is so often preferable to the patent destructiveness of much of the intrinsic navel-oriented anti-science. Let us by all means throw out scientism and scientology but not science. The rational as well as the irrational have their useful function in the human revolution as long as both subscribe to the psycho-social evolution necessary to cap survival with fulfillment. This is equally true for technology and the simplistic denunciation of all technology by the Neo Luddites should also be rejected. Whether we like it or not technology will be required to cure technology, to reduce the scale and power of technology and ultimately to provide the needs of large human populations. It will certainly be a radically different kind of technology, a "softer" technology and wholly subservient to human will and betterment. At the peak of the world youth revolution in 1968 in Paris, students at the Sorbonne University wrote the slogan on the wall, "Let imagination rule!" But the major point is that the way of science and the way of revelation, prophecy, creation and imagination are not irreconcilable but can be reconciled in a revolutionary society.

Appropriate and Inappropriate Technology
THE U.S. AGENCY FOR INTERNATIONAL DEVELOPMENT provides a summary definition of appropriate technology i.e. ..."is intensive in the use of the abundant factor, labour, economical in the use of scarce factors, capital and highly trained personnel; and

intensive in the use of domestically-produced inputs." There are some important problems with the concept particularly those related to efficiency and economics of scale. Thus appropriate technology in certain social circumstances may not be the most efficient in a productivity sense nor the optimal size for minimum cost. On the other hand since we have discounted environmental and social costs these criticisms may not be entirely valid. Thus design for minimal depletion/pollution has side-benefits which are not normally costed. Moreover these diseconomies of scale include social and environmental diseconomies which again are not normally costed.

An aspect of the technology debate which is critical is related to scale and complexity. As technology increases in scale and complexity it becomes more elitist and less amenable to human intervention and participation and therefore more alienating. Scale and complexity are in turn related to centralization and bureaucratization. These reinforce the non-participatory, monolithic nature of high technology. However we must not confuse complexity and sophistication or scale and sophistication. These are vexatious questions particularly when we assert our support for participatory technology. It is obvious we must bridge the two cultures in our formal education system to enhance the level of participation. We will return to these questions in appropriate sections of the book particularly when dealing with proposed solutions.

No matter the kind of technology we propose we must avoid double standards and apply real operationalized and open assessment to all new technologies. Assessment must be an integral aspect of the political process. It must be one of the major information flows that feeds into political decisions.

As we will be soon illustrating our preference conceptually is expressed by the term appropriate technology. The appropriateness relates to both social and environmental goals. Negative impacts are to be minimized. It is a matter of our own bias that we would predict smaller scale and less centralized technologies which, while not unsophisticated, are understandable to most people. Appropriate, of course, also applies to end-use particularly in the case of energy technologies. In order to conform to environmental appropriateness, technologies should embrace durability, life-time efficiency, bio-degradability and materials conservation including reusability and recyclability.

Chapter 3

The Semantic Environment
A Voyage Among Concepts

IT MIGHT BE USEFUL AT the very beginning to provide a simple conceptual dictionary. We are mainly describing a specific type of future society. The various terms used for this future society tend to be pejorative, i.e. conserver society, zero growth society, steady-state society, the frugal society, the paraprimitive society.

In particular the word "growth" even when modified by organic or controlled is inferior to development. For one thing development is multi-facted. For another, human development is the last exponential. Many terms conjure up a vision of radical impoverishment. Although we do find the Science Council phrase "elegant parsimony" felicitous in expressing the new life-style, again we feel "parsimony" is pejorative. Pierre Dansereau's "joyous austerity" and James Robertson's "voluntary simplicity" are also foreboding. Candles and cold baths are not what we must face if we do not choose more growth but rather the ultimate consequence of choosing it. We have been conditioned to mindless consumption despite its costly side-effects to our internal and external environments. We find it difficult to imagine a world without an endless cycle of spending and wasting even as we waste ourselves. At the same time we are assaulted by growth propagandists feeding these fears. And we are equally informed we can have sustainable growth through the power of technology, the same "hard" complex traditional technology which is a central part of the problems that confront and threaten us. We must reject this solution and recognize it as the problem. But we cannot reject all technology.

The various terms used for a new emerging technology

which is (a) low-impacting-socially and environmentally, (b) efficient and durable, i.e. high life-time efficiency and long life-times and (c) under broad human control and accessibility are soft technology, participatory technology, liberatory technology, participatory technology, liberatory technology, intermediate technology, environmentally appropriate technology etc. Still another concept has to do with the stage and process of evolving from pre- to post-industrialism. The terms are usually simple such as growth, economic growth or more or less developed. Again, these are all objectionable.

We prefer four terms which are, at the same time, concepts. These are (1) the sustainable society, the ultimate goal of development, (2) the transition scenario, the path from our present exponential to our future sustainable state, (3) appropriate development, the form of development appropriate to the transition and (4) appropriate technology, the set of tools and techniques appropriate to achieving this transition. While these terms are not free of values their very uncertainty is a necessary platform for dialogue. We must answer the fundamental questions of the meaning of appropriateness, sustainability and what levels of size, development etc. are involved and of course we must agree that sustainability is mutually desirable. The latter seems to have achieved relative consensus almost universally. However there is no consensus on means, levels or paths. The dominant view, based on conventional wisdom, is to copy the future invented by the U.S., a future we have seen and, which we know, does not work. The conventional means are high technology. Even where sustainability is recognized as ultimately inevitable it is deferred or ignored.

In this book it is our intention to concentrate more on the path to the future rather than future itself. It is the political economy of transition that is critical although we will provide a blueprint of the future society. A blueprint, of course, is not even as meaningful in discerning total form as a skeleton. A rich literature on Utopian futures is emerging in which common and converging elements appear particularly those relating to the psychological and emotional needs of people to encourage enrichment rather than impoverishment. Parallel developments have to do with the value of the human bond, of community, of cooperation and of conflict resolution, i.e. with the social capacity of individuals.

At this stage in the book it is time to abandon the analysis of problems and deal with those basic concepts which are central to the solutions we shall be proposing. To begin with we shall attempt to provide an intellectual history of our response, understanding and perception of environment. Critical to the proposals we shall make for a new society which can cope with the essential problems of equity, energy and environment is to attempt to match social and ecosystems. The latter operate in such a way as to eliminate waste and achieve dynamic stability through harmonious symbiotic relationships between species and their surroundings. Sustainability is a natural condition of the natural world although not without exceptions and disruptive accidents. The challenge is for human societies to design their habitats, their productive and consumptive systems and in general their tools, products and processes in such a way as to impact minimally on the environment.

A Generational Evolution of Environmental Responses

THE CONCEPT OF the generational evolution of our understanding, response and approach to environment is necessary to see where we are, where we came from and where we are going. This evolution is both conceptual and operational. It involves changing attitudes and initiated action — legislative, regulatory, administrative and technical. This generational evolution is accompanied by and interacts with a broadening information base which plays a role in refining and modifying concepts, operations, management and informational techniques.

It should be made clear that conceptual responses, precede by a generation or more, operational responses. Moreover, some legislative actions are not truly operational particularly when they are in the form of guidelines or when they specifically incorporate a substantial quantity of time before the guidelines become operational. This leads to considerable delay. This is true for renewable resource management, demand management and technological and environmental assessment.

The first generation is dominated by a combined attack of those various action-directed methods on pollution and is therefore oriented to pollution abatement and pollution control. It is a direct attack on the symptoms of environmental degradation in air, water and soil which have interfered with the proper productivity and renewability of the flora and fauna of the natural environment whether wild or cultivated. It makes little or no impact on the existing techniques or human attitudes. There is no explicit action which promotes environmentally innovative technology or alteration of the habits and life-styles of people to reduce the impact of human activities on the environment. The only function of the first generation approach is to set limits. It is primarily an approach or response which attempts to control and reduce undesirable symptoms of pollution, not eradicate the true causes of pollution. The first generation approach does not question, in any fundamental way, the dominant orientation towards traditional economic growth goals or the almost exlcusive concern with the supply side of the energy-resource equation. Demand is expected and encouraged to increase at a "business-as-usual rate".

This first generation response was still situated within a geopolitical and social context of vision of plenty or the potential of plenty. The Canadian resource forecasts and analysis, proven and potential, were still very large in terms of even the highest projected consumption. We still thought of ourselves as exporters of surplus resources beyond our own need. In the case of energy resources, this notion was established by the various formulations of the National Energy Board. Energy, of course, is ultimately the measure of the accessibility and productivity of all goods and services. Thus an exponential vision of energy source is the basis for a continued euphoria about growth. This first generation was dominant in the period 1970-1973.

A number of geopolitical developments indicate the transition from the first generation to the second generation concept. The Mid-East Oil Embargo of December 1973, the global debates on environment, resources and population, with their conflicting emphases on equity on the one side and limits on the other were evident on an international scale. In Canada the main development was the slow recognition that our perspective of the size of our fossil fuel energy resource base (oil and natural gas) was much smaller than previously estimated — so much smaller, in fact, that our self-sufficiency in these resources became threatened. Some of the consequences of the new geopolitics is the emergence of a new economic world order. The global socio-political agenda has been radically altered.

When the era of cheap oil and gas (cheap energy) ended, combined with the alteration of our exponential expectations for our own energy resources, a qualitatively new generational approach and response to environmental issues emerged. Some of the aspects of this second generation were an emphasis on conservation, a concern for population policies, a dramatic re-evaluation of our export potential of oil and gas to the U.S., and the first stages of policies designed to control the demand for, as well as, the supply of resources.

At the same time a preventative posture began to emerge in addition to the dominant response-to-symptoms approach of the first generation. Assessment of various kinds, embodied in such legislation as the Environmental Assessment and Review Process (EARP) and the Environmental Contaminants Act, are representative of a preventative approach. While these may be limited by constitutional and political restraints they are steps forward.

However, within the context of the political and economic realities of choices, options and actions, the second generation is still basically concerned with growth, supply, consumption, employment and inflation (the traditional economic concerns).

The politics of crisis and dilemma continue to haunt us and because problems proliferate faster than solutions the new global debate on growth forces us to consider a third generation approach. At this stage of conceptual evolution we hypothesize a radically restructured society. The Science Council has identified such a new society in Canada as a "conserver society" and elsewhere as a zero-growth or no-growth society, a "stable-state" or "equilibrium state" economy. We prefer the sustainable society for reasons discussed earlier. We have no clear picture, blueprint or model of such societies. We have no clear understanding of the politics and economics of transition from "business-as-usual" to the "unusual-as-business". Many critics and analysts recognize and affirm that such a radical evolutionary leap will be imposed on us by circumstance at great cost in terms of social disorder, economic discontinuities, dramatic shortages. However, we may still have the opportunity to choose the path of such a transition. Precursors of such choices are appearing in countries like Sweden and Norway, in states like Oregon and even in provinces like P.E.I., but extrapolations of such models to Canada as a whole are not simple and the Chinese extrapolation, while valuable for insight, which some have suggested, seems impossible. Nevertheless we have entered the third generation at least in terms of discussion and analysis.

Concommitant concepts relating to the environment of the third generation are stewardship and "living between limits". The former represents an ethical and psychological revolution in our treatment of the environment whereby our concern is for long-term stability and renewability in order to secure and pass on to the future a major part of the natural heritage we inherited from the past. "Living between limits" means that human activities are controlled so that we supply goods and services at a level above the threshold necessary to sustain our physical, mental and emotional well-being and yet below the limit that depletes our resources or saturates and exhausts the assimilative capacity of waste repositories. Both concepts require quantification and precise definition. The lower limit is easier to define that the upper and steering a course between varying and ill-defined limits, is a monumental task. It may well be that the limits of waste rather than growth are the determining constraints. At the same time we inhabit a planet of sovereign nation-states at widely different levels of development and with great differences in perception, policy and priorities regarding the major issues of resources, population and social change.

The task of enumerating and conceptualizing the third generation is a form of normative future studies. The more immediate task is to operationalize the conceptual elements of the second generation within the context of recognizably necessary change. This leads us to the logic of transition. We stand at the threshold of transition and it is the choice and implementation of the actual path to our sustainable society that is critical.

In conclusion, if we were to use simple and broad characterizations of the three generations of response, they are (1) responsive, (2) preventative and anticipatory and (3) integrative or system change to sustainability. The first two are predicated on continued economic growth but reformed to reduce the costs of growth and to avoid inappropriate growth. The third represents a radical change. The first is reformed historical growth, the second is a technically fixed growth but in the third, growth is transferred almost entirely to the psycho-social environment. The first approaches upper limits rapidly. The second slows down the growth of limits and the third lives within established limits.

It is of interest that conservation may be and is becoming more and more, a central aspect of all three responses. We believe it deserves special merit for analysis. It can merely express a form of the bridging technical fix leading to new stages of growth. It can also be the form of transition to the third generation response of sustainability.

Concepts of Conservation
CONSERVATION IS A FORM of decelerating or levelling-off of growth analagous to arms control vis a vis the arms race. It buys the time essential for the transformation of attitudes and institutions. But more than this it is an exercise in future living, i.e. it develops cultural changes which incorporate those required for a sustainable society. Essential to this first transition stage is that it be a step-wise process proceding in seemingly limited steps but growing by deceptive accumulation over time. Thus the establishing of conservation policy is to prepare for a very major transformation, i.e. a qualitative leap by planned incremental phased manageable steps that inevitably lead us to it. When we discuss the transition to a sustainable society we will return to this aspect of conservation. Now it is important to understand it abstracted from policy.

Accelerated human activity in the securing of food, shelter and the myriad of goods and services deemed necessary to provide the good life has demonstrated its capacity to adversely affect our natural environment. Compounding this pursuit of a high standard of living is the burden of increasing numbers. The ever-expanding scale and intensity of human intervention now seems capable of threatening the integrity of even the largest ecosystem and possibly upsetting some of the great natural geochemical balances essential to the support of all life on this planet. We are faced by a dilemma: the very act of securing our life support systems may be threatening the carrying capacity of our environment.

The only means to resolve this conflict is through management of human activities that have an impact on the environment. Intrinsic to fulfilling this role of steward of the biosphere is conservation of resources and energy. This is the most direct means to achieve conservation of the environment.

Human societies' capacity to survive and flourish depends on continuity of the energy, resources and living space provided by the sunshine, air, water and soil which constitute our life support systems. A resource may be defined as a source of supply, support or aid, especially one held in reserve. In even simpler terms resources are unconverted wealth. This is true of so-called waste. The value of a resource is its capacity to satisfy certain current and anticipated real demand. Resources may be renewable (income) or non-renewable (capital) but even the latter are amenable to some conservation through recycling, reuse and durability. Renewable resources are particularly sensitive to the quality of the environment whose degradation can threaten their renewability. Environmental pollution is a signal which informs us that the ecological systems upon which all life depends are threatened. Nature offers us both environmental goods, i.e. sun, wind, soil, air and water and services, i.e. photosynthesis, natural cycling and even wild life monitoring of degradation.

Priority to conserve will usually be assigned to those resources already perceived as scarce or those seen as depleting rapidly. Little priority to conserve is given to resources with no tangible value or which appear in inexhaustible supply. Unfortunately, air and water have, until recently, been placed in these categories. Nevertheless a rationale for conservation could be arrived at by combining the sciences of ecology and economics. Ecological wisdom teaches us that an apparently intangible resource may be a critical strand in the fabric of mutual interdependencies which sustain all of life. Economic knowledge has taught us that the seemingly plentiful can be made scarce by an exponential increase in consumption.

A combination of these disciplines shows the futility of technological solutions which are themselves ecologically wanting or which require uncertain lead times presenting us with the prospect of sharp intervening social discontinuities.

Conservation is the means of maintaining and restoring ecological equilibrium — a state of mutual interdependence and balance between humans, animals, plants, air, water and soil. Waste is a mortgage on the future, possibly leading to foreclosure. Conservation is insurance there will be a future. The main target of conservation is to overcome or limit the depletion-pollution problem.

The word conservation comes from the Latin and means literally "to keep together". It does not mean rationing or hoarding. It does not imply the ability to define some clear and ultimate limit. Rather the concept of conservation implies the rational management of resources in order to sustain long-term needs while minimizing the negative impacts on the environment. It involves harmony (symbiosis) between human resource requirements and the resource base or carrying capacity of land, air, water and critical materials. It implies the principle of sustained yield. Thus the conservation concept creates a bridge between ecology and economics since it deals with the mutual interdependence of living systems and environments and the allocation of scarce resources drawn from the environment.

A good contemporary definition of conservation is that of Professor Harold M. Rose of the University of Wisconsin who desribes it as "the optimum allocation of natural, humand and cultural resources in the scheme of national development, whereby maximum economic and social security will be assured." Conservation can be accomplished in several ways. One is by doing more with less, — that is, through increased efficiency. It also can be achieved through reuse and recycling, or doing more with the same. Still another form of conservation is through durability, extending the lives of goods and materials. Finally a major source of conservation lies in the use of wastes. More and more, wastes are being viewed as misplaced resources. Support for transformation of wastes for uses that would otherwise require more raw materials is a major aspect of conservation.

The general function of conservation is to extend the lives or decrease the depletion rate of critical resources. The extension of time allows for a more orderly transfer or substitution of other technologies and resources or the development of new sources, all of which requires substantial lead times — during which shortages can be critical. The range and flexibility of technological strategies is ths enhanced by an improved supply situation for a particular demand. Thus conservation policy is supportive of both resource and environmental policy.

Accepting conservation as a sound and desirable policy, the issue becomes the establishment of a program to minimize social costs, inequities and economic disruptions. To conserve without at the same time planning to minimize these disadvantages would not be sound policy. Here we return to the basic definition of optimization of resource use, which requires the resolution of possible economic and ecological conflicts. There is no necessary duality between economics and ecology, between the pursuit of a healthy standard of living, full employment and other economic and social goals and the conservation of the natural environment. It is critical to the survival of our society that these multiple and valid goals be reconciled.

Human societies in order to survive and flourish, require definite life support systems comprising energy, resources and the biosphere. To the extent that we degrade, deplete or destroy these life support systems we threaten our own survival. And in so doing we accumulate a burden of environmental costs — of abatement, prevention or control. To the extent that we secure, extend and protect the basic life support systems we prolong the carrying capacity of our environment. Waste and inefficiency in securing the life support systems degrade the present and threaten the future. Conservation and efficiency in securing, using and disposing of resources are the twin mechanisms for enhancing survival and ensuring the future.

There is an intimate relationship between the cycle of resource-use and the quality of the environment, at each stage in the cycle — exploration, production, transmission and transportation, consumption and waste disposal — there are environmental impacts. Reducing demand and extending supply through conservation and efficiency brings an accompanying reduction in environmental damage throughout the entire cycle. Thus conservation is pollution prevention. But it is also sound economic and environmental policy.

Three basic human control systems may be used for the conservation of the natural environment. These are the legislative process, self-interest and ethics. No legislative system alone, no matter how perfect, can provide full protection. Self-interest, unfortunately, does not always function in harmony with environmental needs. Enlightened self-interest and an operational conservation ethic are required to supplement legal controls. If government, corporation and citizen all adopt the conservation ethic, together we can find ways of resolving the apparent conflicts between self-interest and common interests.

The Sustainable Society

THE SUSTAINABLE SOCIETY IS one in which a dynamically stable human population derives a sustained yield of goods and services from a virtually constant stock of matter and energy and in which the resources are matched to the size of the population to support both survival and fulfillment. Several implications arise immediately. In no case are we describing constancy in static terms but always dynamically. In the case of people, births and deaths go on but the rates are matched deliberately at the lowest possible level for dynamic constancy. The lowest possible level can only be affected by the longest possible life-span. In this case we have a low through-put system which is the most effective to sustain. And in addition all inflows equal outflows.

In the case of physical capital resources we have a parallel situation. There is consumption depreciation, replacement and obsolescence. Again we must aim at a low through-put system where durability becomes equivalent to extended life expec-tancies in people. As also for people we must encourage a low rate of production and consumption. In this system we are matching ecological and economic thresholds, i.e. acceptable rates of depletion and pollution and sufficient carrying capacity for our stable population. Durability and recyclability are essential to minimize inevitable amount of depletion and pollution.

The goal would be to secure as many resources, particularly energy, from renewables. By using energy income sources we intrinsically achieve a very low rate of depletion. If we could develop a solar and harvested biomass source augmented by wind to supply all our energy requirements we would still face both depletion and pollution but at very much lower rates and more to do with support materials and hardware for conversion and transport of energy. Again we would have to design durability in these to reduce through-put and depletion. Even maximum levels of recycling will incur some losses so that incremental increased inflows will be inevitable. Again the search for utilizing renewable resources for materials of construction and the replacement of petrochemical stock by cellulo-chemical stock for plastics, pharmaceuticals etc. would be necessary. The replacement of synthetics with biologicals in general would be the way to reduce depletion.

It should not be any more technologically difficult to design durability than to design obsolesence. If we could aim at an average durability of goods approximately equal to that of people, i.e. between 75 and 85 years we would achieve a dramatic reduction in through-put. The problem is the need to maintain and encourage innovation which would certainly increase life-times of capital stock. A dynamic inventory integrated with innovation would have to be constructed whereby innovations would be based on mutation principles, i.e. the replacement would use the materials of the replaced in a generational evolution.

We will choose about 75 years to achieve the sustainable society realizing the arbitrary and precarious nature of this vision. We shall be proposing not only a theoretical model of a steady-state or sustainable political economy but a theoretical transition or path to it. The truly revolutionary nature of the ultimate sygmoid society lies in its profound change in all the sub-systems of economics, politics, culture and technology. Durability alone confronts the present system with an irreconcilable impact which would destroy it and cause incredible dislocations if it were imposed quickly. But equally impacting are the new notions of the political distribution of power. We will have created a political economy of equitable distribution rather than one of maximization and concentration of production, ʻconsumption and power.

Cultural implications are no less impacting. The variety of goods will most likely decrease radically while consumption addiction will disappear. We will no longer be continuously confronted with ephemeral and synthetic "needs" deliberately fostered by behavioural techniques. But as in the case of politics and economics, if we can avoid Walden II, Brave New World and 1984 in our sustainable future we should be spiritually and physically far healthier, far more involved and committed and living in far greater harmony with ourselves and the finest of our humanist and democratic traditions. Marx's vision of a society in which we have attained the state "from each according to their capacity and to each according to their needs" will have been fulfilled. The notion that incentive would disappear with cooperation and productivity decline with social equality is threatening but could be averted if our new social order is less order and more a controlled anarchy or anarchy within a system of self-imposed controls and being necessary, therefore recognized as another extension of freedom.

Another cultural impact will be that low rates of production may increase leisure time even if there is a return to hand-crafted traditions. We must be psychologically able to use leisure creatively.

We must keep in mind that what we are proposing is for Canada. We must guard against those who will accuse us of freezing global inequalities. It is perfectly true that the organic model of growth is one in which the young (or populations) grow rapidly (exponentially) in roughly the first quarter of their path to maturity. This is equally true for nations. There are many that require rapid but controlled growth simply to reach levels of potential sustainability.

To repeat therefore, the sustainable society is one which at any time offers to human societies, environmental goods and services and both income and capital stocks of materials sufficient for very long-term survival at an acceptable pattern of life. It should be emphasized that what is being sustained are both living entities and the environment in which they live. In particular it allows a particular size of population having achieved stability to sustain itself in terms of its total needs of energy and resources for both the desired quantity and quality of life. Although there are groups and individuals who still cling to sustainable growth as a goal we will reject this. The sustainable society is the conscious adaptation of human societies to the limits imposed by growth and/or waste. It must not only sustain the bio-chem-physical aspects of life at a high standard of health but also nurture the psycho-social and emo-mental development of humans — the last exponential. In the conceptual description given above, the issues of the form and content of the total pattern of living or social system are not decided intrinsically. That is, the issues of centralization versus non-centralization, equity versus dynamic inequity, high technology versus energy income sources, public versus private ownership etc. may not necessarily alter the goal of sustainability. This author believes this to be erroneous when actualized. However it must be acknowledged that theoretically at least, a world of very large numbers (perhaps 25 billion) could be sustained by a high technology source of energy such as fusion or the "self-sufficiency" thorium cycle of CANDU for perhaps a million years. The arithmetic is quite simple. One need only calculate the size of the resource base required to serve the current per capita energy needs of an economically advanced country (i.e. U.S.) apply this to 25 billion people and then decide if there is a match between the expected global resource base and the sustainable population. Both fusion, fission or breeding would have to unfortunately conform to the "law of the minimum", that is one would have to examine this energy system as a total system with all material and energy inputs and outputs and see whether there were not input or output materials or energy which limits growth, waste or net energy recovery. It is highly likely that the resource base is not the limiting factor but other materials or wastes (material or energetic) create real constraints. The constraining factor could be thermal or radiation pollution, critical materials of construction or impact on climate. Preliminary analysis would indicate all of these are much more constraining than the size of the resource base. And, of course, this is the crunch because sustainability in a state of grace would not be concerned with the basis of sustenance provided that truly served the goals of very long-term stability. This nevertheless does not rule out very broad estimates in the size of populations and the levels of consumption at which they may be sustained.

The other questions which assert themselves between the hard and the soft paths to sustainability have much to do with life-style, culture, the shape and nature of economic and political institutions, with services and with the even more fundamental issues of human and social development with its parameters of motivation, involvement, participation, fulfillment, identification, social cohesion and the entire attitudinal and behavioural spectra of human-human, human-Nature, human-machine and individual-society interfaces. But even the posing of these questions carries covert assumptions which affect their answers. For those who believe that technology (hardware and software) is essentially neutral and it is only the purposes to which they are put by society that is significant, and if this belief is accompanied by a theology of technological omniscience then we have an ideology of progress which can marry any available political ideology from the far left to the far right while still embracing sustainability or even indefinite growth. With high technology and unending technical fixes the arithmetic in isolation has some plausability, particularly if we propose that there is a technical fix for the law of the minimum and the second law of thermodynamics. One thing seems clear, that while one may share radical values about equity, i.e. that the equity issue is the most critical and has the highest priority, the argument about which path serves equity most quickly and permanently does not necessarily conform to a particular path to sustainability with equity. This is a critical debate since this author has himself stated that equity and environment are the twin problems which cannot be separated but must be solved together for a stable world in a sustainable environment.

The future like the weather has always been the subject of much talk but questionable predictability the practice of soothsaying, foretelling, prophecy and divination is as old as history. The vocation of prediction not prostitution is the oldest profession. Today the field is more fashionable than ever. The model is America which has invented the future. Gertrude Stein wrote, "We are the oldest people in the world. We have been living in the 20th century longer than anybody else." And someone must have said — we have seen the future and it doesn't work.

One of the major arguments developed in this book will be that the combination of the unique threats to survival has unalterably transformed the course of future studies although recognition lags behind this perception. Now the future and survival have become twinned and even fused. An unprecedented dimension of values now accrues to all future studies and that is the value of the future itself. Willy-nilly the science and art of conjecture finds itself set in the theatre of the crisis of progress, the more so because it has been so firmly attached to the cause of growth. Now the cancer of growth threatens the body politic.

It is a historical veracity that divination and dominion have twinned so often in the past for mutual benefit of the divinors and the "divine". Kings, emperors and other tyrants sought solace and sanction from their court soothsayers for the continued consolidation of power. Often the divinors were cloaked in the garb of religion to provide an added sanction to the established order and its future perpetuation. The future then and now was a gift of privilege. To tell fortunes, to possess fortunes and to be unfortunate is a linguistic as well as a social link.

In post World War II America, in the boardrooms of the mighty, the military, the multi-national and the multiple bureaucracies of government — contemporary soothsayers predicted unprecedented levels of power and growth. Nothing exceeds success and prophets who predicted profits reaped lavish rewards. But the mutual euphoria was not to last.

The previous orgy of technological forecasting with its assumption that automating our life-styles through the application of behavioural technology constitutes progress has not succeeded. We may ask, legitimately, about this period of phenomenal growth. Did the forecasters predict the future or did the trend determine the forecast? We must also question the criteria of success since economic growth was accompanied by the growth of degradation. Mounting social and environmental costs, many yet to be paid for, and the accelerated depletion of resources certainly allow us to question this net cost effectiveness. Nor can we count the costs of alienation, emotional and mental damage or many other ravages of degradaton of social and physical environments. The obsessive selection of growth indicators with deficit budgeting of social and environmental costs is part of the conventional progress paradigm. Thus the criteria of success is built into the assumptions of the value of growth.

The uniqueness of the contemporary threat to survival has changed the agenda of the future, altered the script and vastly increased the cast. We must now all ask who sets the agenda? Who writes the script? Who does the casting? As long as the answers remain that our present institutions structurally geared to blind growth are directing destiny we are locked into a losing game.

In testimony to the great impact of the Club of Rome's global studies many countries have begun to take more than just a second look at growth. Many European countries are examining models of qualified or organic growth. Canada has a major government sponsored study on the Conserver Study. Sweden is already planning the transition to zero energy growth. The Chinese experience seems to look more and more interesting. The Ford Foundation, the Rand Corporation and this author have established the credibility and viability of low energy growth through conservation and efficiency. Some of the scenarios of low energy growth indicate the practical possibility of reduced nuclear expansion in the next 25 years. Nothing illustrates the inherent distortion of policy than the U.S. and Canadian blind commitment to high nuclear growth. The view that there are no energy alternatives to nuclear fission and fusion represents literal accomodation of the huge industrial and military investment in nuclear power.

The apostles of continuous energy consumption growth into the long-term future manage to ignore the law of entropy. Weinberg and others have calculated that we are less than a century away from a level of consumption representing a significant fraction of total solar incident radiation. The limit here will be unacceptable impacts on global and regional climates. The barrier to sanity as Weinberg so perceptively notes is that what is everybody's problem tends to be nobody's. Energy policy, health protection and environmental protection all ilustrate the bankruptcy and crisis of planning. And in the planning process the predictors have played, wittingly and unwittingly, a role of accomodation. If scientists are going to make "Faustian Bargains", let them not make them in the name of humanity.

Other aspects of the game of prediction are the communality of belief between the proponent and his hired prognosticators. Not only is there a shared value system but there is also a shared belief in a mystique of techniques and the cult of the expert. On the one hand credibility becomes an exclusive function of credentials and methodological complexity and on the other we have the elitist accomodation to the system. The cynical academician or the professional may appear to sell his services without believing in the game but there is a natural gravity towards rationalization. The net effect is that the advice that is being sought is gained and both vested and self-interests are sanctified. What is being sold, of course, is the system. It is no accident that there is a current fashionability in the application of complex methodologies to predicting the future. Part of the techno-scientific mythology is its belief in its own mythology camouflaged as methodology. Another part is a belief in the direct proportionality of effectiveness and complexity. This is somewhat marred by a critical examination of policy and decision-making. While these are certainly the subject of legitimate scientific research nevertheless real decisions and policies are surprisingly simplistic and predictable. The system acts to perpetuate the system and to maximize its strength. Strength is synonymous with size and therefore it is the rate of growth that is the ultimate measure.

It is quite clear that future prediction or forecasting for all its trappings of scientific methodology has served the deceptively simply purpose of the growth paradigm. The future as an extension of the American dream became the fashionable tool of industry, government and the military.

Fortunately a new wave of future concern and commitment is now directing the present. Survival as a threat in the future is becoming a critical force in the social and technological decisions of the present. More and more this purposive and normative projection is asserting itself over the fashionable extrapolated futures.

Chapter 4

Canada: The Investment Colony
A Historical Perspective

A Mini-History of Canada

HISTRICALLY CANADA WAS BORN out of war in which one nation, the English, defeated another, the French, in a prior existing colony of the latter. Both were preceded by long periods in which indigenous peoples occupied the land. Colonial status remained, only the rulers changed. By accident the country to our south was born out of a revolution against being a colony of these very same English. These two historical facts plus the geographical nature of Canada shaped its future. The role of the Mounties then and now has been a monument of non-accountability.

Canada is a federal state bordered by three oceans and covering a huge territory some 4000 miles from coast to coast and several thousand miles from the U.S. border to the Arctic. The largest proportion of population is clustered in a group of metropolitan centres strung out along the full width of the country and in a strip some 100 miles deep. The topography climate and soil quality of Canada are extremely variable. Industrial development and population are largely concentrated in Ontario and Quebec. The mid-West comprises the bread basket while Alberta and British Columbia are rich in resources of all kinds. The country is a mosaic of ethnic and racial groups, as well as of resources, so much so that wide disparities exist between peoples and regions.

When one includes the indigenous peoples, Canada is clearly multi-national. Added to this diversity are conflicts between federal and provincial jurisdictions usually over disparity or the accidental distribution of resources. An acute conflict exists over the issue of whether Quebec is a nation rather than another province.

Despite having economic indicators of high development, the Canadian economy is more characteristic of those states that are only approaching economic development. This is reflected in our truncated, resource-based, branch-plant industrial development.

We have never managed to resolve the conflicts of a federal state born from a concept of confederation which is now clearly redundant. In particular, the emergence of environmental and resource problems, which are trans-boundary and supra-sovereign, create a gross mismatch between our constitutional and political systems. Within this scheme of mismatches there is little legislative and jurisdictional basis for a national resource and environment policy. Ultimate control of the land and its resources are vested in the provinces. Within this jurisdiction land use is further vested in property rights of individuals and corporations. With the exception of "waters where fish abound", navigable waters, transboundary transactions and federal lands including north of 60 degrees, the federal government has no control over the use of land. One result is a serious rate of loss of agricultural land as it is converted to non-agricultural uses.

Even where federal authority exists there is no unified land policy and the net result is that economic and political imperatives dedicated to short-term returns consistently tend to defeat environmental and resource concerns. Each federal department attempts to maximize its own rate of return or extension of power. The federal Department of Environment (DDE) is emasculated by limited jurisdiction and by having been combined with the Department of Fisheries, which is often more concerned with economic and political motives not consistent with sound resource management. The DOE is big on migratory bids but small on almost everything else. It is even castrated in its capacity to impose legally mandated limits on various pollutants unless these have received prior certification by the Department of Health as constituting a threat to Canadian public health. The case of sulphur dioxide is a perfect example of the castration of the DOE and gross omission by Health.

The World Health Organization has recognized that sulphur dioxide emissions are one of the most serious global contaminants. Epidemiological studies abound in establishing correlations with this pollutant and respiratory disease. The INCO plant in Sudbury and the tar sands plants in Fort Mac-Murray simply get away with murder. The result is an orgy of guidelines, rather than mandated limits, for most pollutants; guidelines which do not guide and which rest on the assumption of good corporate citizenship, a myth of the first order.

Internally and confidentially Environment Canada has

adopted the advanced principles of (a) the polluter pays; (b) the use of the "best available technology" for pollution control; and (c) the burden of proof shifted to the polluter. In practice all of these principles are consistently violated within the existing legal system. Even where the regulatory agency fails to regulate their failure remains outside the law. At least in the U.S. there is the possibility of legal action against such dereliction of duty.

Added to thse problems are several other myths. Chief among these is that Canada is rich in resources — renewable and non-renewable, so rich in fact that we have huge exportable quantities. This myth has led to tragic export policies, with fossil fuels and uranium, and could extend to renewable resources including protein. There is an illusion that the carrying capacity of our land is far greater than our population. Thus a second myth is that we are under-populated. This myth is accomplished by a simplistic arithmetic that divides land mass area by people and disguises the distortions of population distribution. The fact that most of our land has no carrying capacity and that we consume everything on a grand scale is also glossed over. In terms of consumption, for example, our 22 million people consume all critical materials at a rate equivalent to that of 660 million Third World people. At the same time that we are resource imperialists we are also pollution imperialists, contributing a disproportionate amount to the global budget of environmental degradation. Thus the "tragedy of the commons" (Garrett Hardin) is revisited internally and in respect to our global role.

Jurisdiction disputes are real but also encourage the game of jurisdictional juggling whereby problems which are everybody's become nobody's. On the other hand, the new resource republics — Alberta with its oil and Saskatchewan with its uranium — act as if they have been preferentially blessed by an accident of geography to exploit these resources by themselves and for themselves. The ugly game of geopolitics has been internalized in the politics of Canada.

If Canada has a tragic flaw it is none of these problems, profound as they are. The flaw lies in the nature of our political process which places a high premium on ministerial confidentiality and discretion, cloaked as responsibility. We have an unending series of mini-Watergates, mostly concerning hoarded information that was not disclosed. We are a closed society without legal or operational rights to information that is controlled at the top. We have neither the form nor content of participation. Despite the virtually continuous embarassments of secrecy, which inevitably are disclosed, we do not seem to learn and we are reluctant to change. Despite lip-service and tokenism to participatory democracy, accountability and accessibility, we continually permit hoarding, distortion and manipulation of information. The posture of almost all governments at all levels is to deny information, then to deny revelation and finally to be found guilty of both. If we can manage to open the closed political process in Canada we will have taken the first and perhaps most critical step towards creating a consensual future.

We have referred to the multi-national nature of Canada. This would certainly include the various distinct nations of indigenous peoples, potentially the present Province of Quebec and possibly several regional groups ranging from the Maritimes to the western provinces. But we would insist that a multi-national pattern could only be meaningful if all groups agree to subscribe to and abide by certain principles. In terms of the norms of self-determination and sovereignty we realize that such principles are not usually a prior condition for nationhood. But we realize equally that nationalism, per se, as the sanctification of limited but totally discreet sovereignty, is exactly what prevents the peaceful achievement of planetary stability. Nationalism creates a basic mismatch between environmental and political jurisdictions. As an alternative we are proposing to optimize the political and national aspirations of legitimate groups with environmental and resource imperatives. To simply allow the Balkanization of Canada for the lesser purposes of pure independence without recognizing and cherishing mutual interdependence would seem to be in nobody's interest. In effect we are not denying Quebec's right to separate, but we are extending the P.Q. proposal of separation within Canada beyond postal and customs union and common markets to the commons of ecological principles incumbent on all parties. Cultural determinism alone remains inviolate as the right of each. Cultural diversity has its own values which we cherish. However to be inter-dependent we will have to communicate and thus even within culturally distinct groups language capacity will be broadened and hopefully we will become universally bilingual by choice.

To maintain the notion that each group's autonomy extends to the wilful abandonment of the principle of stewardship and equitable sharing of all resources, regardless of geopolitical distribution, would be simply to confirm Canada as a microcosm of the disunited world of conflicts in which nobody ultimately wins and all ultimately lose.

Prior to the considerations of multi-nationhood we should face up to the realities of existing vulnerability through foreign ownership. A separate Quebec would no more have effective mastery over its own economic affairs than does Canada at present. Canada can only be understood particularly in its development history through understanding the role, control and penetration of foreign investment.

The Repatriation of Canada

WE HEAR MUCH ABOUT the repatriation of the Canadian constitution from Westminster but we are even more in need of repatriating our economy from Washington. Ultimately we may have to expropriate and nationalize our resource industries in order to avoid depletion and to restructure our economy. Our half-hearted attempt to establish a competing fossil fuel corporation, Petrocan, is the typical "too little too late" posture. Buying into Syncrude was little more than a bailing-out process. The full significance of our branch-plant, resource oriented economy is that it robs us of the capacity of determining the course of our own development. It disarms us in the critical R and D function and makes us technologically dependent. It also imposes a course of development on us which is largely counterproductive. We have too long clung to the myths that venture capital is what we need and that we can only find it outside of our own country.

We canot blame the U.S. for her dominion over Canada. It was largely at our begging invitation. Our national accounts vis a vis the U.S. have become tragic. Resource development capital has largely flowed into Canada from the U.S., to secure resources for the U.S. economy and return a host of derived products with large value-added content. The outflow is not simply resources, however, but huge amounts of interest, management and licencing fees, royalties, advertising and insurance charges, engineering, design, patent and consulting fees; all of which compound our problems of inflation and balance of payments and reinforce our branch plant status. Not only is inflation catalyzed but also we suffer permanent unacceptable unemployment. (5% is unacceptable socially despite government policy to accept it) and permanent trade deficits in labour intensive secondary industrial products.

An even more curious feature of our branch plant character and over-reliance on a single trading partner is that a large part of our trade is between subsidiaries and their controlling external corporations. This relationship presents special problems of covert expatriation of profits in the form of a variety of unaccountable services provided by head offices.

It is fascinating that increased reliance on primary resource industries has actually decreased employment. For example between 1950 and 1970 mineral production tripled in Canada, gross annual fixed capital formation leaped from $148 million to

$1 billion while employment increased from 120,000 to 128,400, i.e. production increased 300%, capital formation increased by 700% and employment increased by 7%!

In conclusion, the Canadian economy has been based on the wrong exports and imports, creating a powerful distorting force in traditional economic development.

When we examine the details of our economy the real tragedy emerges. The examples of folly are legion, so much so that our policy seems to have been a CARE program for the foreign multi-nationals (sometimes masquerading as Canadian companies either by name changes or the addition of "Canada Limited" to the name, e.g. Imperial Oil is 70% owned by Exxon).

For example, if we examine leasing, licensing and royalty rates on our vital resources we find incomprehensible and unwarranted give-away programs. Royalty rates are the legitimate form of pay-back to the country for the privilege of foreign exploitation of its resources. It is meant as serious profit sharing not token payments. The effective royalty rates on Syncrude and GCOS range from 7.5 to 13.2%, the lowest in the world. North of the 60th parallel our royalty rates are a ludicrous 5% for the first three years and 10% thereafter compared to Alaska North Slope royalties of 20%. Norway's royalty rate reaches 76% of gross revenue from some of its North Sea oil and gas (developed by some of the identical companies that operate in Canada).

Every acre of our tar sands has been leased at $25 per acre for the first five years and $1.000 for the next sixteen years. Most of the leases have been arranged with foreign companies. By contrast the same companies paid the U.S. government hundreds of thousands of dollars for leasing oil shales (these are even less attractive from a net energy point of view).

In the period 1965 to 1968 oil and gas companies in Canada paid taxes on only 5.7% of their profits. Shell Oil in the period 1964 to 1969 had profits of over $½ billion without paying one cent in federal taxes (it actually received $4 million in grants). Between 1965 and 1971 Imperial Oil paid an effective tax rate of 19% on $1.526 billion of "declared" profits. Trans-Canada Pipelines showed a profit of $110 million over a seven year period without paying one cent in taxes. All of this was reported in the Carter Royal Commission who declared "Oil and gas industries have long been enjoying unnecessary exemptions". One wonders how these same oil companies which made acceptable profits at $3.00 per barrel are doing at $13.00.

A fascinating source of information on the foreign ownership of Canada is provided by the Corporations and Labour Unions Returns Act (CALURA). Considering that effective control can be wielded by 25% ownership, some 21 industrial sectors in

1971 were foreign owned, ranging from petroleum and coal (99%) to beverages (32%). Only services, leather products, retail, furniture, construction, agriculture, forestry, fishing, clothing and utilities are controlled by Canadians (over 75%). Computers, aircraft, oil land, coal, tobacco, transportation equipment, mineral fuels, chemicals and automobiles are foreign controlled by 80% and over.

In 1971 the assets of foreign controlled corporations rose by $4.6 billion to $54.6 billion. This represented 36.6% of the total assets of all non-financial corporations in Canada. There are at least 8000 foreign controlled corporations in Canada of which 4304 had over 95% foreign ownership. Total payments to non-residents in 1971 increased by $186 million to $2.239 billion. Of the total outflow, interest accounted for 24%, dividends 35% and "business services" for 41%. Other payments in royalties, advertising, research, insurance, management fees etc. have all increased dramatically since 1965. The average asset size of foreign owned corporations is about four times the Canadian controlled company. Non-Canadians actually owned 353 of the 625 companies in Canada with assets over $25 million. This is the essence of branch-plant status. And even Canadian-controlled companies pay large dividends to non-residents.

The major inference of this situation is that economic and industrial activity in Canada is directed by outsiders for purposes which are those of outsiders. This orientation robs Canada of the capacity to manage its own development. External forces, not directly concerned with Canadian development needs, shape our industrial activity. U.S. controlled subsidiaries in Canada shipped 83% of their total exports to related corporations and purchased 76% of their total foreign purchases from their own subsidiary or affiliated companies. This incest is at the expense of any meaningful Canadian development. In 1971, 90% of the dividend payments made by foreign subsidiaries left the country, i.e. $542 million. Of significance is the fact that between 1964 and 1971 Research and Development service alone paid to foreigners increased from $98 million to $134 million.

Since 1971 the situation has worsened. In 1973 the total capital outflow from Canada was $4.105 billion, of which "business services" accounted for $1.516 billion. This heading covers a technique to export profits. Foreign firms operating in Canada, between 1960 and 1970, exported $2.625 billion more than they brought in. And most of this was between related corporations. Saskatchewan bit the bullet and almost swallowed it over potash take-overs and the P.Q. has made noises about asbestos. But Johns Manville, the prime target, seems to have escaped present aims.

Canada should institute regulations which maintain clear Canadian control for all foreign investment in Canada. At the same time we should gradually and equitably repatriate large portions of foreign owned industry, particularly resource industries. Japan and Norway, for example, have continued to attract foreign capital despite having far more stringent controls than Canada. A reasonable access to our exportable resources by those who really need them should be part of our international policy and this principle should not necessarily exclude the U.S.

To Separate or Not to Separate

THE CURRENT CANADIAN identity crisis is not going to be resolved by referenda or elections in Quebec or at the federal level. No matter which way such votes may go, Canada will remain divided, not only between Quebec and the rest of the country, but also between provinces and regions. Canada is in reality a multi-national state. The indigenous peoples of Canada are composed of several nations.

There is every theoretical reason to concede that the French-speaking people of Quebec have all the characteristics of a nation. Quebec represents a geographical, political, cultural and psychological community. This quartet of characteristics represent the essential of nationhood. Economic viability, the argument most frequently used to discredit the separatist movement, is not an issue of nationhood. One might as well question whether Canada itself is economically viable separate from the U.S. One would hardly have withheld the right of nationhood from the old colonies of the great powers because of their economic dependence before and after they shed their colonial status.

The qualities possessed by the Quebecois and many of our indigenous peoples is self-identity and a unique culture. It is the twinning of these two concepts of culture and feeling, within a geographical community that is the irresistible seed of national identity.

However, acknowledgement of the right to self-determination does not constitute approval of nationalism. There is a fine but significant line between nationalism and social cohesion. It is the past absence of this very community of goals that has made nationhood in Canada as a whole more form than content. What we have today is a series of resource republics in Western Canada, an over-developed American industrial society in Ontario, a combination of Brazil and Cuba in Quebec and less economically developed regions constituting the Maritimes and Mid-West. Thus we are a microcosm of the world — Alberta as the Middle East, Ontario as the U.S., British Columbia as

Australia and even the equivalent of some Third World nations in our indigenous peoples. In this way the problems that divide Canada are those that beset the world. The problems create the challenge. A solvent Canada which has resolved the conflicts of multi-nationhood, regional and social disparity, inequities of class, group, sex and race will have created a survival model for the entire planet. A Canada that can achieve an operational unity and overcome the divisive forces of nationalism, spurred by gross inequities, will represent an achievement of initiative.

For a country that has never discovered itself, has never experienced a truly national consensual emotion, except perhaps over hockey, the threat of disintegration over Quebec's separatism could lead to discovery of a new identity. The problem is that there are hard-liners on both sides who are indulging in the dangerous game of creating chaos in the belief that it serves their ends. Such people are blind to the costs of their reinforcing prophecies; they play the "prisoner's dilemma" game, an illustration in game theory based on the opera La Tosca where everybody loses when each one plays to win. This is a game for losers only. Everybody will lose is such an approach is used. The people of Quebec will pay the first costs while Canada itself will pay the final cost.

Despite our acknowledgement of the reality of multi-nationhood in Canada and the unquestioned right to self-determination, a solution should be sought which would maintain and sustain a collective identity without sacrificing the diversity of culture. We believe a consensus might be found around this goal but there must be a dedicated search. In order to reduce the uncertainties we are proposing the following shopping list of principles for the building of a multi-national state.

1. Unity is intrinsically superior to disunity. Fragmentation is an invitation to the loss of identity, not to its achievement, in the geopolitical context of North America.

2. Nationalism is essentially a divisive force once historical self-determination has completed its purpose. Nationalism is susceptible to mismatches in political and ecological sovereignties. The biosphere has no boundaries and the problems of its maintenance can only be solved when there is a better matching or jurisdictions. This is also true of more limited ecosystems or groups of ecosystems. Thus while the right of self-determination to nationhood is a principle, its exercise at the expense of ecological sovereignty is a violation of principle.

3. Equity and sustainability are the two major issues in Canada and the world. Both issues must be served and solved, for without the former we will kill each other and without the

latter we will murder the earth. In eaither case early winners will be late losers.

4. A uniform homogenized culture is neither viable or desirable. There is strength and wisdom in diversity. We should promote diversity while reducing disparity to levels where there is a conscious choice of the mix of the quantity and quality of life chosen by each group. This essentially is a principle of ecological diversity fostering regional authority in choosing various trade-offs, i.e. between environment and economics, energy and environment and equity and environment within broad ecological constraints. It also represents the principle of optimizing independence and interdependence, negating neither. Mono-cultures of any species including humans are extremely vulnerable to extinction and large-scale disruption. It is Mao's thousand flowers policy.

5. Quebec is not just another province. It never has been and may never be. Quebec comprises a geographical community, a political community, a cultural community and, most powerful of all, a psychological community. These are the necessary requisites of nationhood. All this must be acknowledged if we are to negotiate. Nations can be born into association as well as separation.

6. The BNA is redundant, not just because of Quebec, but because the world and Canada have changed so radically since 1867 that the BNA has lost relevance.

7. A negotiated settlement of the issues of Quebec and other nations and regions in Canada would necessarily require the relinquishment of some sovereignty by all actors in the negotiations, including the federal government, the provinces, the indigenous peoples etc. None of these actors could retain all the traditional rights of separate nation states.

8. Good marriages and good divorces can only be made between equals. The basic necessity for joining in common cause is the state of equity. It is also the acknowledgement in advance that separation is an option whose right cannot be questioned. On the other hand equity does not necessarily mean one-dimensional uniformity, i.e. perfect economic equality in the narrow traditional sense of economics. It would mean, of course, equal access to services, to health, education and justice.

9. Confrontation cannot resolve conflict except by mutual or preferred destruction, not a solution in any case. Conflict resolution can only be achieved by a series of integrative negotiated stages in which the rules of the game itself may have to be changed if they obstruct the resolution.

10. Purely political and jurisdictional conflicts satisfy and reinforce psychological needs which may be spurious. Achieving

a "right" is merely a preface of the validity with which it is exercised. These are never substitutes for resolving the truly significant issues of survival, peace and equity and the removal of threats to their maintenance. As long as the struggle for "rights" are motivated exclusively by hostility and aggression they remain rooted in negative goals or become exclusive goals unto themselves.

11. In recognizing the truly unique cultural dimensions of Quebec we should have faith. Quebec will choose to become bilingual or multi-lingual through its own internal forces when recognition of its right to self-determination is granted legally and with full acceptance.

12. Quebec poses unique problems to the rest of Canada which that province must recognize fully. Complete separation and severance is impossible. Both sides cannot maximize their own demands.

It is important to accept that only good will is required immediately. All else is negotiable. Negotiations take time and the conflicts will not be resolved for many years.

This is where the ecological imperative must assert itself. Environment will not go away if you ignore it. The urgency of environment and resource questions demand early answers. While we are negotiating to settle the new divisions of jurisdictions we should agree not to defer these other issues. There are serious institutional and attitudinal obstacles to the solution of resource and environmental problems. We cannot even plan the solution until we plan to remove these obstacles. What is most required is a phased plan of transition.

The Canadian Unity Task Force has moved in general along the lines of the solution this author is proposing. The co-chairpersons, John Robarts and Jean-Luc Pepin, seem to accept the so-called concepts of "special status" and the "French fact". Pepin's phrase "Third Option" has already drawn pot-shots from Trudeau.

It is a shame that a Canadian solution should be bargained for in the time-worn traditional way of each side asking for more than it would settle for in the assumption that both sides view each other as unwilling to compromise from the very beginning (which unfortunately could be true). We do not believe the Quebec referendum now planned for 1979 will provide a definitive answer to the national unity question, and that is why we would recommend a people's commission to develop a consensual formula for an association which is less than Levesque's but considerably more than Trudeau's.

A people's commission, not a Royal Commision but a commission of non-royalty composed of our most creative and dedicated Canadians from every walk of life would be the best approach. This commission would be joined by a common bond of dedication to conflict resolution, dialogue and the maximization of justice. Citizens unencumbered by political affiliation or the rigidity of bureaucratic roles could best hope to create a dialogue. Such a commission could set out to repatriate and reconstitute the constitution with a view to recognizing Canada as at least bi-national if not multi-national. The task of redividing powers and reassigning jurisdictions is monumental. It could be simplified by an initial agreement on principle relating to basic internal and external policies of continental Canada, representing consensual goals. The problem is a miniature replica of the global dilemma and because of this a Canadian solution would have immense significance for the entire world. We are proposing a solution to the contradictory nature of Canada which can be expressed by the concept of the sustainable society. But the critical problem is to describe a peaceful and low-cost transition. It is the staged and phased transition from the present to the future that is at once manageable and necessary.

Chapter 5

The Political Economy of Transition

The Transition Strategy and the Sustainable Society
THE KEY TO THE fulfillment of the program described herein is the implementation of manageable steps comprising a path to the sustainable society, i.e. the path from an exponential to a sygmoid society. The sustainable society (conserver society) is the only means of achieving long-term survival. All growth societies are doomed to collapse either through limits of non-renewable resources or limits to waste. The transition strategy has five major components:

1. Maximization of efficiency in the use of all resources, particularly energy, whether supply, conversions or consumption — largely achieved through software improvements in resource and energy demand management, maintenance and operating efficiency etc. This simply draws upon the inventory of available techniques for resource and energy management. Dow and Dupont, for example, have been so successful in this form of conservation that they are selling their know-how as a service.

2. An incremental slow-down in actual or real per capita consumption of resources creating a slow-down in through-puts that is a decrease in the rate at which goods are produced and consumed; this could be effected by enhanced durability and re-cycling. However, this should be accompanied by a program that ensures a more equitable distribution of goods and services.

3. The phasing in of necessary changes in the inventory of existing attitudes and the capital stock of hardware technologies) i.e. the development of a conserver ethic and lifestyle and the introduction of conserving technologies.

4. The democratization of the policy and policy-making

processes and the release of all hoarded information particularly that which is relevant to resource and energy planning.

5. Development of coherent energy and resource policies integrated to population and social policies generally and achieved through a high level of consensus regarding short, medium and long-term goals.

By applying the above components the transition period may be divided into three stages of development. The first stage will contain an exponential, but significantly decreased growth rate (1977-1987). This has been characterized as the efficiency or technical-fix stage. The next period (1987-1997) will involve largely linear growth, projecting lower demands at the end of the period than in stage #1. The third stage will be an inverted exponential curve, i.e. the upper branch of the S-curve ending at some steady-state optimal mix of population and consumption that is sustainable for the very long-term. The total time for this stage to stabilize could be between 28 and 53 years. This third period could stabilize through an entirely new phased transition — a reverse S-curve to a stable-state at a still lower growth consumption level. Excess capacity can always be applied to global equity and thus it is wise to plan the first transition at some higher level of sustainability than may be ultimately necessary or acceptable. The above time horizons correspond closely to numerous scenarios developed in Canada, New Zealand, Denmark, U.S. etc.

The first step in preparation for the transition period should be an inventory of national resources — human, institutional, renewable and non-renewable. An independent assessment of global efficiency in energy and conversion technologies, particularly energy income sources, should be made. Cost-benefit analyses and environmental and social impact assessment should be extended to include a maximum number of internalized social and environmental costs. The accounting systems used should themselves be open to assessment. A second but equally important step would be to examine and quantitatively describe the national energy system, including energy flows within consuming sectors, between regions and across international borders. The first step will test the hypothesis of sustainability, the second, the potential of conservation and efficiency.

Social Implication of Transition
BROADLY SPEAKING the transition to sustainability in Canada involves deliberate and phased transformations in our economics, politics and culture, and a pervasive change in the system of values which govern our personal and social lives. Difficult problems intercede between the now of consumption

and the then of conservation.

The human dimension is a fundamental part of the transition period. How do we retain self-identity and self-interest without being selfish, and at the same time discover group identity without group-think or the subversion of self? Interwoven with this apparent dualism of individuality and sociality is one concerning freedom and responsibility. How can we protect the freedom of conscience and creativity in the face of the impact of social constraints designed for group survival? Must we abandon traditional personal freedom, recognized by law after centuries of social struggle?

There seems little doubt that to survive in a world of shortages we must avoid the "tragedy of the commons" in all senses. But surely this avoidance cuts across the grain of our entire socio-political and cultural systems whereby we are programmed to maximize our share of the commons, i.e. the environment. Do not the enterprises of a survival society necessarily destroy the existing rights of property and profit? Will not these new enterprises transform the power of the price and market systems? Surely these transformations can only be an end and not merely a means if we are to avoid the costs of major social disruptions. The answers to these basic questions all converge towards an accordance of Hardin's principle of "mutual coercion, mutually agreed upon" but this convergence is itself an aspect of transition.

All of the above tends to lead to a political-economy of transition which is essentially mixed. Such a political-economy has elements of private and public sector activities in peaceful co-existence, and elements of labour and capital in meaningful partnership. The cultural forms of the transition will also be mixed, with a gradual, but meaningful, shift in life-style.

But these necessary shifts in our society must be catalyzed. They would occur much too slowly through self-generated or evolutionary means. The catalyst can only be education in all its forms and through all its structures, techniques and media. A new Utopia cannot be imposed. It must be chosen. To participate in the choice we must become informed. Information in the hands of citizens can be the weapon for change. Achieving a new level of education appears a manageable political task, although our political process is geared to oppose both freedom of information and the right to become informed.

Despite this plea for consensual maximization and pluralistic politics we must make some hard choices. The time has come and passed when we can tolerate the official "tragedy of our commons". We have no choice but to nationalize and socialize air, water, soil and the critical resources necessary for survival.

We are not talking about old ideologies in new trappings. This will not be a form of the old or new left both of which are steeped in an ideology of progress, of scientism and linear modes of thought. We are not denying rights of private property as long as this property is not an essential part of the commons. We are denying the right to enact the tragedy of exploitation. Private enterprise need not disappear if it is ecologically sound and responsible. Nor do we wish the bureaucratic state to become the ecological authority replacing the bureaucracy of power and exploitation. The people will own the commons and they may rent it but never relinquish the right of recall. Where the lines are drawn between the rights of property and the ecological imperative is itself open, negotiable and part of the transition.

The politics of transition includes the phased withdrawal of the rights of private property where environmental goods, services and critical resources are involved. The politics of transition also includes the phasing out of centralized bureaucratic decision-making institutions in favour of a decentralized system. We will have to reconstitute the BNA ACT and we may well see the dismantling of the present provincial-federal system into a multi-regional form of decentralized authority.

The politics of transition must put particular emphasis on strategies to reallocate resources to renewable, recyclable and reusable forms. This reallocation will undoubtedly involve deliberate interventions or distortions in the price system, using a combination of "carrot and stick" incentives and disincentives. It will be important to maintain the principle of equity, that is equitable distribution or distributive justice in the disincentive process so as not to punish the poor or less wealthy. Pricing should more and more reflect real costs, particularly where social costs have been subsidized, deferred or discounted. This means that price should reflect total lifetime costs including those that are now externalized, i.e. paid for by society as a whole or by future societies.

A particular problem area is the transportation sector both in terms of economic impact, energy demand and social and environmental impacts. The change from private to public transit will be a critical problem of the political economy of transition because the automobile is entrenched in life-style and central to our economy. Another problem on the labour side is shifts in jurisdictional areas where less energy and capital intensive but more labour intensive substitutions are generally introduced. In all such cases protection of in-place labour and capital interests should be maximized so that first choice in shifting jurisdiction or investment should be offered to existing power structures. The goal should be to create a null sum zero game situation in which there are no losers, only winners. Poker is the classical sum zero game in that the sum of losses and wins equals zero. This requires a high level of planning and the patience to promote phased change with deferment of the normal gratification of quick returns. Removing the threat of social dislocations to special interest groups would decrease their resistance to necessary change.

The goals of the transition scenerio are straightforward. Firstly we must use the next 23 years to become informed and involved; to maximize the number of actors who decide and create the future. In accomplishing greater involvement we will have altered the political process itself. Secondly, we must shift the inventory of attitudes — individual and corporate — to embrace an ethic and mode of existence based on consensuation.

These two primary goals are no unrelated. There is a dynamic relationship between them and they will act on each other. It will be our hope that the first two stages of transition, i.e. reduced growth will prepare our minds and our institutions for the final stage, i.e. steady-state equilibrium or zero growth. This could conceivably evolve to an even lower level of conservation. The precise consumption level of this final stage will be based on the principle of sustainability, i.e. sustained yield and availability of necessary resources. Inverted exponential growth may be a necessary later stage. The advantage of such negative growth would accrue from material surpluses for disposal to the cause of equity.

The task of unravelling a complex system of sub-systems, all reinforcing an internal dynamic geared to growth and positive feedback, seems almost impossible. In part this is because we juxtapose the present reality with a future picture. Once we can imagine a gradual and smooth transition from the present to the future, reaching our goal becomes more feasible and less impossible. The key policy which can enable this transition is energy conservation. The face of energy is the portrait of society — its institutions, life-styles and values. And yet the conservation option does not confront the existing system with radical and unacceptable changes which it cannot contemplate. The adoption of the conservation option will naturally lead to the necessary transformation of the inventory of capital goods and attitudes. We will have a form of a "withering away of the state" of growth and consumption addiction.

The Nature of the Economic Crisis

HAZEL Henderson, Herman Daly, Georgescu-Roegan, Kenneth Boulding and others have described the multiple contradictions of our present economic system. Put simply these are as follows:

1. High complex technology designed to stabilize the free market and the democratic process in effect creates the reverse trend. It requires social subsidies while becoming incomprehensible to society. It demands elites while catering to public support. It becomes vulnerable in proportion to its power and monlithic structure.

2. Complexity and laissez-faire principles are incompatible. The concepts of a free dynamic market operated by invisible hands cannot exist within the complexity of a modern industrial state requiring as it does far greater increments of planning and of making meaningful choices available and pervasive. Bureaucracy needed to run the system defeats participation that would make it acceptable.

3. The supposed trade-off between employment and inflation is not only the source of cyclical crises but is no longer, if it ever was, true. Real inflation is being caused more and more by soaring social costs (added to GNP as though they were socially positive instead of negative). It is also being caused by the inflating cost of energy supply as substitutions themselves are more costly and often equally vulnerable in supply. We have noted this in the substitution of nuclear for thermal power.

There is also a broad crisis of the failure of distributive justice in our system. We hide injustice under averages. We mask dislocations by labour procutivity statistics in industries which by nature are capital and energy intensive creating the social burden of structural unemployment let alone social pathology. Volunteer work, education or household work are viewed as free goods, much like air, water and land, having no economic value in our society. If we added up all the real value created by some 5 million people contributing a year of meaningful work this is equivalent to $50 billion (not measured in GNP). On the other hand we probably have paid social costs of this order which are included. That we should measure GNP for a fat system including the fat and the funeral services for death by obesity is a farce or as Ralph Nader has said, "Every time there is an automobile accident the GNP goes up." War is even more productive.

The ultimate paradox is, of course, that high rates of traditional development has not created nor can it guarantee the just society. On the contrary it has made injustice a permanent feature of its life as it has unemployment, inflation and social pathology (let alone cancer and a degraded environment). We have now entered the period which may best be presented as a crisis of crises, i.e. a simultaneous convergence of monetary and psycho-social inflation, environmental disruption and resource-depletion. Hazel Henderson calls this the "entropy state"; the new economic order is disorder. This is a state of unmanageability wherein the costs of transactions (management) of every kind exceed the total value of production, i.e. the cost of bureaucratization exceeds the value produced. The exponential of social costs exceeds that of real growth in goods and services, i.e. externalities exceed internalities. The result is not merely stagnation but deterioration, a structural and system state of crisis. The body politic and economic is suffering a terminal disease, not properly diagnosed or treated. The real "tragedy of the commons" may well be psychological, i.e. "problems that are everybody's are nobody's". The market which is no longer free even under rampant capitalism cannot properly allocate scarce resources. This means traditional or neo-traditional economic theory is itself in crisis. Profit usually means that someone profits while society pays, i.e. it does not reflect real costs or real values.

Centre-stage in the clash of paradigms in limited fields or current world views is the fundamental question of the meaning of *value* or what we value or even better what we really value through choice. Individual freedom and collective security, the private and public right confront each other continually because there is no unified value system which mediates between the valid aspects of each. The same conflict exists between spiritual and material values, between genuine lower-order needs for survival and higher-order needs for fulfillment.

Rate and magnitude leaps in technological complexity appropriate increases in control and management. Only the cost remains inappropriate.

It is fascinating that certain fashionable concepts of the '50's and '60's have simply become moribund. The whole idea of the post-industrial society in which information becomes the largest industry and services greatly exceed goods (Daniel Bell) or the leisure society in which automation significantly displaces people or the super-technological state of the more benign but still technocratic (Buckminster Fuller) or the excessive success of extrapolated futures (Herman Kahn) have either become shadows or departed the stage of global debate. We adhere to the reality of the knowledge explosion but we do not buy the rest of the package.

Howard T. Odum has proposed a sort of energy currency in which all productive activities will be dynamically modelled in terms of energy and matter flows. The focus is on net energy analysis, those processes with the greatest output/input lifetime ratio at minimal environmental cost would be most profitable. But the system requires the conversion of power to money and this may contain hazardous assumptions. Moreover neither money nor energy (power) can cost non-quantifiables. These must still appear in cost-benefit and risk-benefit analyses but the currency is values and principles and the time-frames may be vastly extended beyond strict quantification of the distribution effects to a large degree what we cannot quantify we should reject if risks are large and we have the luxury of other options.

We have argued previously and repeat here, that both capital and income resources should be publicly owned. That this is not easily or immediately achievable should not deter us from facing up to the issue. In the transition periods we should take the first step of establishing two operationalized principles. These are (1) accountability and (2) responsibility, and both should be integrated into the political process as democratic rights. Governments must have the basic resource data in order to plan and in the case of capital resources must be the exclusive explorer. This is necessary so that when "rights" are turned over for private development the leasing arrangements can guarantee the fair distribution of profits.

We should introduce a broad system of resource allocation, mandatory where possible and designed to be equitable and optimal, not an easy task. Equitability should certainly be geared to real need.

We should possibly carry our allocation principle further to include an entire variety of critical resources which face enhanced depletion. The most equitable way might be the so-called "white rationing" whereby every single person in the country over 18 would get ration coupons for gasoline for example whether they were drivers or not. Drivers could purchase ration coupons from non-drivers, thus rewarding those who are less tragic in their behaviour towards the commons. The total ration coupons issued per month would be geared to the target consumption. This would be the ultimate control on depletion.

The above system could apply to population control as well in much the same way. But the area of coercion is certainly far more sensitive and society would have to achieve a high order of consensus that a ceiling on population perhaps by 2025, would be desirable.

In general the present system of incentives, taxes and subsidies mostly directed to encouraging rapid exploitation and growth should be reversed and new incentives, taxes and subsidies introduced to encourage conservation, recycling, waste utilization and the shift to an energy income base while discouraging waste, depletion and capital and energy-intensive programs. The entire taxing and pricing system should deliberately favour durability, life-time efficiency, the minimization of social and environmental costs, the decreased depletion of critical resources and full employment. This is a primary but necessary reform.

The vast increase in productive services employment of all kinds is critical to restore lost and losing security in the large urban centres of Canada where the delivery of regular and emergency services lags seriously behind the congestion of activities and the traffic of people and materials. Advantages are that many of these services jobs are labour-intensive while being neither capital or energy-intensive and they have low to no environmental impacts.

At the same time we should increase all programs designed to improve the quality of our environment including the built environment. This should be a policy of repair, maintenance and conservation, not new developments where these are speculative or socially unnecessary.

The existing societal tools of anticipation such as environmental and technology assessment, "employment impact statements", "carrying capacity" and the prevention of new and recall of old hazardous chemicals should be broadly exployed. For carcinogens and mutagens broad use of the Ames test should be entertained. As we have stated earlier, however, all assessment processes must be given the power of prevention and thus must be open and accountable with provision for public input.

A Menu of Measures to Achieve Sustainability

TO SUMMARIZE, SOME specific social measures which must be taken to complete the political economy of transition are:

1. Universal freedom of information; accessibility to and accountability by all institutions. This in itself is not sufficient and the Canadian government would have to initiate a vast campaign of public education on all major issues and on the future in general. A national 3 year teach-in utilizing all communication forms could radically multiply the number of actors in the theatre of the future.

2. Concommitant with the above would be the universal process of open hearings and ultimately referenda on all major developments including the future itself. The Berger Commission approach is a good start. Funding for intervenors must be socially borne and equal to that of proponents.

3. The first act of a guaranteed annual income must be instituted applying in order of priority to all those actively seeking work, to housewives and students. Funding would derive from the savings in energy supply development and withdrawal of military capacity. Our first analysis indicates this could be about $10 billion per year for the next 22 years.

A generalized annual income (GAI) is a mutual contract

between government and society insofar as those who are not gainfully employed or making socially useful contributions (students, home-makers, etc.) agree to guarantee annual responsibility through voluntary or make-work programs. Thus GAI is at the same time a state of full employment.

GAI will be gradually extended in each phase of transition aiming at zero unemployment by or shortly after 2000.

4. In the first two phases of transition we should reduce our military budget by 75%.

5. By the end of the first stage we should have completed a new constitution and negotiated a settlement with Quebec along lines discussed in the previous chapter.

6. Our goal for 1990 should be inflation and unemployment rates of less than 5% and by 2000 we should aim at close to zero for each.

7. We should begin the task of indexing all goods (producer and consumer) by a ratio which reflects optimum durability and life-time energy costs.

8. By 1990 we should have implemented a Fault-Free Compensation Act for all industrial diseases. At the same time our Food and Drug laws, environmental and health regulations should eliminate the worst of carcinogens, mutagens, etc. and begin the phased withdrawal of all highly toxic substances. A large retroactive assessment would have to be made and all new substances thoroughly assessed. Safety would have to be socially determined.

9. We should establish a very large national energy corporation ENERCAN which can begin the task of truly creating a viable energy supply industry; the Office of Energy Conservation should be expanded tenfold and funded appropriately; dramatic changes in the mandate of utilities, in rate structures and in incentives to conserve and disincentives to waste should be introduced.

10. Early in the second phase we should complete our national futures teach-in having utilized the first phase for the equitable distribution of information and the right to become informed.

11. Stage #2 will see a more rapid extension of public ownership of resources without eliminating the private right to operate (but not to own).

12. Stage #2 should see the broad improvement in the durability to life-time energy cost index to 150 by 2000.

13. Population growth should be restricted to 1% per year on the average divided in some equitable way between excess births and immigration.

14. By the year 2000 we should have achieved universal

college education for most of the population with a vast increase in retrofit education, to stimulate a conserver ethic and lifestyle.

15. Early in the first stage we should establish a large Institute of Relevant Studies (IRS) with a broad mandate to research problems and search and reach solutions.

16. The third stage of our transition scenario should see zero growth achieved and a dynamically sustainable level reached. Durability to life-time energy costs should reach 300 (indexed at 100 for 1978).

In the realm of political changes we should aim for a high level of decentralization within a consensual scheme of broad goals of sustainability. In the first phase we should alter the political process so that no person can serve as Prime Minister or in the Cabinet more than once and that each term is 6 years. Towards the end of the second stage we could begin real consensual politics by developing a single non-party government with radically new constituencies (non-geographical) i.e.NGO's (non-government organizations, trade unions, industrial and professional associations, minority groups, universities etc.). Perhaps this would be the first fully operational Canadian Values Party.

17. Factory management should be radically democratized beginning with all public corporations.

In the thrust towards decentralization, self-reliant communities of all types would hopefully emerge, such as rental communities, barter communities, neighbourhood industries, cooperatives of all kinds.

18. A vast increase in cable education television should be introduced in the public sector with self-programming facilities for the user.

The Institute of Relevant Studies among other things would direct itself to a scheme to produce a universal and complete food UCF, possibly in the form of a universal class of food i.e. a biscuit designated as the Canadian Peace Biscuit and designed as a crisis food for the starving and hungry.

In general there must be a high level of coordination between the phasing in and phasing out of all these measures with a strong commitment to equity for those phased out. There would be a vast shift from goods to services and a radical reduction in the variety of goods but quality criteria would also radically increase. Leisure may well have to replace jobs as consumer goods are decreased and this will entail a revision in the concept of leisure possibly directed towards universal higher education.

Many of these provisions will be further detailed in the following discussion including some attempt to assess the obstacles. There is no intention of providing a formula for successful transition but rather to present a broad and open menu which is not exclusive.

There is a further group of critical issues which were dealt with in the previous chapter which have high priority, i.e. Quebec, the repatriation of Canadian industry and the reconstituting of our moribund constitution. But of prime importance is the reduction of unemployment. To a large degree this is related to energy and other recommended policies. An accelerated conservation/renewables and make-work program with its redefinition of work are all part of our proposal for a guaranteed annual income (GAI).

We must withdraw from NATO in the first stage of transition and this must be done gracefully and with careful explanation to seek sympathy for our grand experiment. At the same time the first stage must redistribute information radically and institute the right to become informed universally.

We should possibly seek alliances of non-alignment and also divest ourselves of many other vestiges of the sovereign state in a non-sovereign ecological reality (see last chapter).

Energy Policy for Transition

ENERGY POLICY IS CRITICAL if not central to the political economy of transition. For this reason we have chosen to deal with energy in a separate chapter (following). Nevertheless at this point it would be desirable to consider certain broad principles of energy policy that relate to our phased transition.

To begin with we wish to assert that energy conservation is not merely one of many options but rather a necessity and, in the longer term, the most economical and ecological of energy choices. To a degree we examined conservation conceptually in Chapter 3. At this point what is of paramount significance is that the conservation potential and its implementation path coincides with and and reinforces the multiphased transition to sustainability. Thus the full conservation potential falls into three generations which reinforce or even catalyze the generational evolution of social ecology. The transition which we are recommending is one from our present anti-ecological state, socially and biologically, to one in which social systems are patterned on ecosystems.

Generational Evolution of Conservation Programs

THE RATE OF implementation of conservation measures is controlled by a number of factors such as the rate of replacement of capital stock, off-the-shelf versus new plant, process or management technique, the economics of retrofit and the

77

system of incentives and disincentives for stimulating conservation, some of which involve systemic changes. In general we are proposing a three stage conservation program in slightly advanced phase to our general transition scenario. We do this because conservation is the key to successful transition. The time frames are 1978 to 1985, 1985 to 2000 and 2000 to 2035 and the conservation potential is accelerated in each time frame. We are adopting the strategy of an Accelerated Conservation Program (ACP) (See Widmer and Gyftopoulos, Technology Review, June 1977).

In summary, therefore, first generation conservation programs are the off-the-shelf, good housekeeping, energy management techniques together with those other readily available, immediately implementable, add-on or retrofit measures with high payoff savings such as insulation etc. First generation will also include a segment of new plant and process, i.e. new capital stock where available technology with more efficient energy utilization or conversion and lower life cycle costs may be introduced.

Second generation conservation will be largely focussed on improving second law efficiency by more careful matching of energy source and end-use, by the beneficial use of thermal discharges (district heating, waste heat generation plant, etc.), by broad utilization of organic wastes as fuels and by significant development and application of biomass, solar and wind sources. By the year 2000 the aim would be to have renewables supply 20% of total primary energy. This period will also witness the virtual abandonment of central electrical generation and a vast increase in on-site generation (on-site would represent about 40% of total generated electricity by the year 2000). This would mean an average growth in electrical generation over the entire 22 year period of about 2.8% per annum. A pinnacle of second generation conservation would be industrial-urban-integration as previously described. There would be no operating nuclear plants.

Third generation conservation would see a further major leap in second law efficiency and the universal application of the best available technology for energy effectiveness in the total capital stock. Retrofit district heating would be virtually universal where old housing still remained. The end of this period would coincide with zero energy growth very likely at a reduced per capita consumption, possible equal to that in 1970 or less. Population, of course, would also have to stabilize.

Of particular significance is the improvement of efficiency, particularly second law efficiency with its large potential for improvement. First law efficiency (FLE) (derived from the first law of Thermodynamics on energy non-destructibility) is exclusively concerned with maximizing conversion and not with the question of "energy quality." Second law efficiency (SLE), on the other hand, is concerned with the concept of entropy, i.e. with the notion of quality degradation and end-use matching. The fundamental idea is that energy per se is never consumed, i.e. used up but what we do use is "available work" and it is this we attempt to conserve. The concepts are subtle but powerful in their implications.

We should aim to a national average second law efficiency for the entire energy system of about 50%. Renewables would now supply more than 50% of all primary energy with solar and biomass dominating. Synthetic crude, heavy oils and coal would still be significant fuel and feedstock sources. In all cases central de-sulphurization plants would be used and gasification and liquefaction of coal would provide clean fuels to augment biomass fuels or provide feedstocks.

The Political Economy of Transition

AS WE HAVE BROADLY described, the transition period is one of phased adjustments from the present to the future, so, our recommendations for economic policy are designed in this manner.

Generally speaking there must be deliberate distortions in the price and market system, itself distorted, to correct the present disastrous course. However, people must be put first and the primary task is to seek full and meaningful employment, while significantly altering the meaning of being gainfully employed. This may involve a guaranteed annual income which might be financed in large part by savings through conservation, reduced environmental and social costs (those that were up for payment or being paid) highly reduced military budgets and, to a great extent, repatriated profits and royalties.

While effluent and emission taxes are intended to use market mechanisms for the reduction of environmental impacts they are highly subject to political lobbying or lack of political will to enforce. Unless the penalties are very large and strictly enforced and in the case of unacceptable risks, disallowed, they cannot be successful. Nevertheless experimentation in these taxes should be undertaken and so should tax incentives for pollution control and the development of pollution-free design.

Herman Daly has proposed a system of annual depletion quotas to be auctioned by governments. Daly suggests this would be more efficient than strategies of efficiency or pollution taxes. The basic issue is to reduce the depletion of the capital stock of resources.

Japan has begun to experiment with a new complex indicator, Net National Welfare (NNW). This should be extended to where we subtract gross national pollution in all forms — physical, biological and social from Gross National Product (GNP). But GNP itself will require new concepts of cost, price and value and in particular will have to include all investment in human resources or by human resources, i.e. from schools to households.

The preliminary and yet significant analysis of Mazur and Rosa ("Energy Life-Style", Science Vol. 186, 15 Nov. 1974, pp. 607-610) is an indicator of the value of new indicators. They did an analysis of correlations between national energy consumption and 9 health indicators, 7 education and culture indicators, 7 general satisfaction indicators and 5 economic indicators for 55 countries (available from U.N. statistics). The results are intriguing. While there is a threshold of energy consumption below which there is a clear positive correlation with all the life-style indicators there is a transition level of consumption (for clearly identified economically developed countries) above which there is no longer significant correlations. In other words, above a certain level of energy consumption further increases do not improve life-style (quality and quantity of life). In many cases negative indicators actually increase with energy consumption suggesting there may be an upper limit above which disamenities exceed amenities. It may well be that countries with less than half the energy consumption per capita of Canada have a higher quality of life without sacrificing quantity. Almost all socialist and communist countries have superior health and education distribution.

This study requires amplification and further quantification. There are indications, for example, in epidemiological studies on the impact of life-style on health that peoples living in non-market economies, i.e. far far down on the scale of economic development, have cultural factors stimulating health. These studies also indicate how Westernization of their cultures enhances certain diseases including psychological disorders.

Not only do we require expansion of the social indicator movement but we require that more meaningful indicators *actually* direct our decisions.

A multi-regional country federated around new fundamental principles internally and externally but allowing a very high level of regional decision-making and diversity has more survival value than homogenous centralized monocultures. Since we reject homogeneity on principle we do not propose a Canada unified around false principles and purposes. The problem is to create independent diverse decentralized regional authorities but committed to high levels of interdependency in terms of the most urgent problems of equity, environment and energy. The problem is to create a sound marriage between equal but different partners in which equality itself is a variant of choice.

In this new system or groups of systems what happens to the cherished conflicts of left and right, of labour and capital, of old and young, of men and women. These have political, economic and cultural dimensions and will only be resolved by new arrangements in which the conflicts disappear or are radically reduced. The "necessary revolution" or evolution is also a revolt is also a revolt against orthodox revolution, a revolution against conventional wisdom of all kinds. Traditional ideological differences are no longer highly correlated to solutions to all the most urgent problems. The left is left with promise of equity which it has undeniably achieved to a large degree. But our revolution is one that attends to the problems of equity, energy and environment. Environment remains the neglected problem of all ideologies. At the same time almost all existing political systems seem to agree on a monolithic view of solutions to the energy problem, nuclear power being the major option.

Modern capitalism and modern socialism both equally eschew bigness in business, in government and in production. Bigness is truly a diseased form of administration in that it inevitably becomes alien to the real needs of people. Bureaucracy becomes an ultimate diseconomy of scale in administering the very large organizations. It becomes clumsy and vulnerable, inflexible and removed. This is as true of big business as big labour. It is unfortunate that labour in becoming big has lost sight of its early development when its struggles incorporated the whole spectrum of social reform and justice. Today the very big trade unions and their associations have become more and more like big business, i.e. consumed by the exclusive struggle for power and an ever larger portion of an ever larger pie. There are locals and even unions who do not share this tendency. There is growing awareness among the rank and file that labour should be distinct from capital in its goals and values and not merely economic ones. It is to be hoped that labour will return to its earlier tradition of concern for a broader aspect of social justice without sacrificing its rightful struggle for its fair share of the spoils, conscious always however that the "victor belongs to the spoils." It is a wasteful conflict for labour to be pitted, not only against business but against society as a whole. Corporations on the other hand need not retain grotesque excess profits that could otherwise flow to workers, shareholders and taxes to repay government for assurance. The excessive salaries of certain individuals should be excessively taxed.

81

The realization of this kind of system rests to a very large degree on the abandonment of bigness and the development of a far more decentralized system of governing and producing. Enterprises should abandon the pretext of profit maximization for their shareholders, always pictured in their promotional advertising as the "little people". They are said to be not only little but multiple and purported to own the majority of shares, a clear and unequivocal lie. Of course there may be many small shareholders but they are helpless, not informed and not involved and not in control.

The dismantling of the nation state, i.e. the creation of an anti-nation, has three major thrusts. One is the rejection of the value and need for national sovereignty in its anachronistic form. The second is the dismantling of internal political sovereignty historically derived from traditional forms of party politics, political processes and ideologies. The third is the dismantling of economic sovereignty resting on the notion of the rights and duties of ownership permitting exploitation without social accountability or restraint. Central to this latter issue is who owns or can own land, water and air for the purposes of exploitation. The political economy of transition must lead to a transformation in ownership from private to public sectors.

Sweden has tended to lead the world in many ways, not least of which has been its public airing of most of the issues discussed in this book. Sweden has debated the nuclear issue, proclaimed a nuclear moratorium and fought an election over it. Sweden has planned and debated an ultimate zero-energy policy. Sweden has emerged still dedicated to growth but asking fundamental questions such as is growth possible or consistent with the depletion-pollution problem.

Two Swedish government members of the Secretariat for Future Studies have proposed radical consumption limits on critical resources, i.e. meat and petroleum. They have also made an even more radical proposal, i.e. to take the ownership of all automobiles out of private ownership and maintain total public control. This would be replaced by a public rental system to be used only for medium range travel. It would also be accompanied by totally restricting private autos in city centres and replacing these with efficient mass transit.

Public sector corporations listed on the share market and really practicing industrial democracy and instituting a genuine abandonment of maximization of profit and a genuine distribution of their profits to workers and shareholders could act as models of these new types of institutions. Management would be democratized not only internally but externally. The corporation's "books" would be open to the concerned public.

There are at least three traditions which incorporate these principles and we should attempt to draw upon all. There have been excellent models of industrial democracy in the socialist countries. The co-operative movement and the unions which are oriented to serve their members or customers are two; the limited but dynamic examples of small enterprises which have involved workers in profit and management are yet another valuable tradition. Sweden, Norway and Yugoslavia have successfully employed such measures.

In order to have a controlled system that is not inflationary, that continues to attract enterprise and investment, i.e. that rewards risk, that protects and serves all the actors in the enterprise, requires a highly planned system. The techniques seem available but like conservation or solar heating the obstacles are attitudinal and institutional. That is why the kind of economic system pictured here must result from a transition rather than sudden birth. Problems will still abound in that democratic choice should always be preferred to imposed controls but the former takes more time than the latter and the latter suits the elitist and paternalistic attitudes or traditional control systems. This is not to question the need for very complete legislation for consumer and worker protection despite the threats and protestations of capital. The philosophy of free enterprise is that controls, i.e. interventions in the "perfect" market system destroy both freedom and enterprise. Since these are sacred such destruction leads ultimately to more misery for everyone. Only the freedom of capital to invest and grow is proposed as the means of producing less and less misery for everyone. The fact that this has not and is not happening is ignored. The fact is that the difference between rich and poor is growing and the equity problem has continued to elude Canadian society. Yet basically our policy is to support producers rather than consumers as though these are pure polarized choices. But this thinking is the tragedy of conventional wisdom. On the other hand the welfare state which extols bigness is also a tragedy. There is more real distributive justice in the welfare state but the system also stagnates from bureaucratic pollution.

Economics is a social science in a state of crisis. It has created concepts that are as alien to the real world as phlogiston was to combustion. There is a dire need for a new Keynes of the steady-state whose revolutionary concepts will destroy the dying paradigms of the post-Keynsian synthesis. In particular our economic system has become so mismatched with our ecosystems that the costs of growth, normally obscured, deferred or otherwise externalized are so large as to threaten the continuity of life itself. More and more the concept of harmony and symbiosis must guide us from our personal to our largest social systems, i.e. to the planet itself. We subscribe to Meserovic and Pastel's concept that we must undergo the "eventual transition into sustainable material and spiritual development of mankind" i.e. the path of "organic growth".

The technological traffic problem, i.e. the lag between technological growth and its institutionalized control, is a universal attribute of over-development. Not only have rate and magnitude problems come to dominate the threats to survival but big organizations have created bureaucratic congestion so that the ability to act thoughtfully is itself impeded. Thus both technological traffic and bureaucratic traffic exceed the control systems that would allow the dejamming of social systems. Traffic jams now dominate social structures and technological systems. We are reaching what Hazel Henderson calls the "entropy state" of zero mobility. Even viewed cybernetically the system is overloaded, mismatched in phase and message, filled with lock-in malfunctions and clogged channels. Since power is the source of power the existing power structure does no more than increase the concentration of power. This is true of our corporations and unions and our government.

The result of this congestion is a vast increase in alienation, scepticism and a feeling of hopelessness. Big government, big business, big unions and big science are remote, dehumanized and dehumanizing. Politics is more and more viewed with scepticism, as a dishonourable profession. The corporation suffers an acute credibility crisis. The Watergate syndrome has become universal. We merely watch each new revelation and in the process become insensitive to the significance. The system has failed but most of us nevertheless accept it because part of the failure is that the system has disarmed the people, psychologically, politically and intellectually. Only a radical redistribution of power within the principle of equity extended to the planetary level holds out hope for survival with dignity and fulfillment. More and more we return to the need for a political-economy and culture of transition which simultaneously treats the most urgent problems of equity, energy and environment.

While in our transition scenario we are not proposing take-over, we are recommending the phasing out of foreign ownership and the phasing-in of Canadian control. This will require some tough new legislation applied to financial corporations to shift their loans to Canadian corporations now predominantly going to foreign corporations, the mandatory requirement of independent Canadian public interest directors to be placed on the board of all foreign corporations, the repatriation of covert and excess profits now flowing out of Canada etc. But most of all we require a rational development plan which integrates all aspects of our social existence and which is dedicated to evolve to a sustainable society. We are not denying the complexity of this exhortation. We are affirming that it is the only hopeful future we can contemplate. In the case of the most flagrant foreign owned resource companies whose peformance is so clearly out of line with Canadian interests we should nationalize, paying a fair price for their market value. We should totally repatriate federal territories, i.e. buy back all leases north of 60 degrees. We must create one extremely powerful federal corporation in the energy field. The base of this would have to be the nationalization of one of the existing multi-national oil companies. This should be vertically integrated so that we are in the energy business from exploration to sales. This corporation should become a model of conservation and direct the use of non-renewable materials for appropriate development, largely as a bridging energy source to a renewables future.

International Commitments

ALL "EXCESS" RESOURCES should be directed towards a massive program of constructive foreign aid for the world's poor. We should phase out export of non-renewable resources to the economically advanced countries which are not actively pursuing a dramatic reduction in growth and evolving their own sustainable society. We should concentrate on the transfer of self-help technology, viewing aid in resources as a necessary interim policy to be phased out as quickly as possible. We should concentrate on aiding a few countries to very significant levels through the transfer of appropriate development techniques which are also intrinsic to our own development. This policy conserves resources. By developing energy income conversion technologies that are appropriate to our evolution to sustained yields we can modify, adjust or scale to make these appropriate to the needing countries. This new type of technology transfer must be done through consultation and cooperation with recipient countries.

We are aware that food and energy self-sufficiency are critical for the poorest countries. We should concentrate, therefore, as a deliberate contribution, on food and energy technologies appropriate to the hungry nations whether these are also appropriate to us or not. Actually, low-cost protein-rich culture-free foods such as single and multiple cell proteins will be needed in Canada as well. No aid to the poor should be directed to countries where we cannot assure proper distribution to the people. We should immediately cease our hypocrisy of "aid" with profits since this is counter-productive and self-defeating.

The Unjust Society

WHILE WE ARE preaching the proverbs of altruism and the sharing of our gifts with the unfortunate we should remember that the less fortunate are right here with us in Canada. By any terms, i.e. "real poverty" or "legal poverty" we have some 5 million people who are poor whether visible to our eyes or to our statistics. Some 2 million children under the age of 16 are in this category and the first renewable resource we should maintain are these children. In a country with such a high "standard of living" and so much official self-esteeem, there are over 500,000 dwellings without hot water. Over 1 million Canadians are inadequately housed. Well over 1 million Canadians are over 65 and are treated as non-returnables, throw-aways whose lives are impoverished by neglect, pitiable sub-threshold pensions and inflation. Actually we are an aging society, about 10% of our population is over 65. We need a geriatric revolution as well as a youth rebellion. The poor under 16 and over 65 constitute almost 3 million deprived people, and this in a "just society". And to this we must add the huge number of poor women, the working poor and their families.

And the myth that a bigger pie is the path to re-distribution would be ludicrous if it weren't tragic. Between 1965 and 1969 the poorest 20% of Canadians had their share of total individual and family reduced from 6.2% to 5.6% while the 20% of the wealthiest had their share go up from 39 to 40%. Canadian GNP grew 35% since 1969, yet there has been no significant redistribution of wealth. And those living below the poverty line pay a higher percent of their income in tax than those above. When we turn to our indigenous peoples the tragedy is multiplied. For every white child that dies before the age of 2, eight Indian children die. 80% of all Indians live in sub-standard dwellings while the unemployment rate among Indian males who seek work is 58%. Only 8% of Canadian Indians complete high school. 78% live below the poverty line. Actually 47% of all Indian families earn less than $1000 per year. For 60% of mixed races average annual income for males in $400. The average life-expectancy of the Canadian Inuit is about 24 years.

When we view the waste and inappropriate spending of Canadians in the light of the extent of poverty it is simply disgusting. Liquor sales and betting total $1.5 billion per year. This money could feed 65 million children for 5 years. We spend more on military bands than on all mental and emotional disease research.

Among the most significant changes in the relationship between capital and labour would be worker rights in the workplace environment. Workers should be guaranteed the right to withdraw their labour without repisal when there are unacceptable hazards in the workplace environment. Workers should be guaranteed the right to monitor the workplace environment independently of all other interested parties. Fault-free compensation should become universal, with the burden of proof shifted to the employer, i.e. the onus to prove that contaminants in the workplace environment did not cause the disease should be on the employer. There is ample evidence that the costs of making workplaces non-hazardous are not unacceptably high and can be absorbed without a radical increase in costs in most cases. Laws should be enacted that ensure that costs for health protection are centralized without passing these on to the consumer. If this is not possible then production should be discontinued as substitutes which are less hazardous are introduced. Again, experience indicates that this is feasible in most cases. A radical reduction in the number of hazardous substances that enter the environment is a basic requirement for enhancing public health.

At the same time serious consideration should be given to reducing the exposure to hazardous environments by a combination of a life-time reduction, i.e. through rotation of employment to less hazardous conditions plus a reduced work-week.

In this intervening period of some 23 years much higher levels of industrial democracy should be sought, with more profit and management sharing by workers. In particular, labour should develop its own scheme of participatory epidemiology, i.e. where each worker takes independent measurements of conditions and effects in the workplace environment. The tests can be rationalized and made available for independent assessment parallel with corporate and government testing or hopefully in cooperation. By preparing each worker to be able to continuously monitor his own workplace environment we have radically enriched the data base. There is already a model for this in persons all over Canada voluntarily feeding daily records of weather into the national meteorological network.

As we phase out the most hazardous chemicals, particularly carcinogens, from use it will be very important to study and assess the lingering and latent impacts. Participatory epidemiology will be an effective tool to broaden the entire monitoring and inspecting system and vastly increase the reliability of records. It will be an important aspect that workers keep life-time records of their work experience identifying the nature of hazardous exposures, the life-time of exposure, the levels of exposure and relevant aspects of their life-style, i.e. cmoking, diet etc. They then develop a life-time commitment to the care of their own bodies. These life-time records should be readily retrievable for analysis perhaps by deposition in a central registry. Again there are models for some of this type of activity although not for full participatory epidemiology as described here. In general complete detailed life-time record-keeping should be mandatory with employment in the case of exposure to hazardous substances. Paramedical occupational health training should become universal.

One should not simply accept the continued need for such exposures. Anticipatory techniques whereby hazardous contaminants are eliminated by prior assessment is a far better and less costly posture. Certain kinds of testing for carcinogens and mutogens, such as the Ames test, might well allow us to deregulate the most hazardous of these substances in our environment at reasonable cost. We should place the acceptable level of exposure to cancer-causing substances at zero or the lower limits of measurability. If we cannot achieve this level we should withdraw use of the substance. Whether it be vinyl chloride, asbestos or any other carcinogen there is sound experience that exposure could be reduced to very low levels at reasonable cost. With such chemcials as PCB's and PBB's we must simply use substitutes, as is being done in other countries. Highly toxic pesticides should be eliminated despite claims for cost-effectiveness. These claims are disputable in any case since they parallel the arguments about the relative costs of solar and conventional energy systems, i.e. they compare a mature, mass-produced technology supported by a huge research and development program costed by an accounting method which discounts the future and the unpaid social and environmental costs with an emerging much more benign technology without all that institutional support. Given the appropriate support, biological controls for pests, solar power systems and biodegradable non-toxic substitute chemicals could become economically viable. An intervention into the price system could help facilitate this, i.e. by pricing the full economic, scial and environmental costs of products. Capital would soon be diverted into products of lower cost when the market reacted adversely to the high cost of socially undesirable products or projects.

Some Survival Strategies
THE PHENOMENON of the systemic failure of technological systems is well-known. It seems in part to be a function of complexity and monoculture. The more complex a technological system be-

comes, the more amenable it is to unpredictable and unprecedented types of failure. Ironically such a system often also
becomes more amenable to acts of malice. This latter phenomenon is well-illustrated by plane hijacking. An ordinary knife can
subvert a 747 jumbo jet.

The domino effect as in the failure of the North-East grid
and more recently New York City's black-out, was simply not
expected, nor did it seem amenable to prior safe-guarding. The
vulnerability of nuclear power plants to acts of malice is tacitly
accepted in that none of the numerous reactor safety studies
have dealt with this problem.

There is also a counterproductive aspect to the very attempt
to deal with the problem of acts of malice against centralized
complex high technologies. Increased security can only be
accomplished at the expense of increased constraints on
traditional freedoms, i.e. a greater invasion of the privacy of
technological workers, and perhaps ultimately by the "garrison
state". And even then we cannot be sure who will guard the
guards.

In all technological phenomena there is a clear tendency for
technological traffic to outpace technological control and
regulatory systems. The unique phenomena of "rate and
magnitude problems" are an inherent aspect of the vast increase
in technological traffic. This is true for chemicals, autos,
weapons and nuclear fuel cycles. Moreover, the rising costs of
control and regulation erode the fictitious economic advantages
of many of these technologies. The economic order could not
maintain itself under an adequate system of control of
technology. The irony is that it cannot maintain itself with an
uncontrolled system which only leads to disorder. This is the
systemic failure of the entire economic system. Deficit and
deferred budgeting reinforced by large social subsidies has
created a heritage of false accounting in which new costs of
growth continue to appear and accumulate in the future.
Environmentally induced disease is a prime example of the
present system, but so is the vast increase in psychosocial
pathology and increased symbolic and existential manifestation
of violence. Both structural and unstructured violence are
accelerating.

It would appear that only a significant decrease in the levels
of centralization and complexity, accompanied by a significant
increase in diversity, flexibility, i.e. a significant reduction of
"rate and magnitude problems" through decentralized diversed
flexible scaled-down systems can help. These systems must
nevertheless attend to the real needs of present and future
populations. One of the greatest uncertainties is there are no

viable or plausible models of such non-extrapolated futures or more important models of transition, describing paths of least social cost from the present to the future. What we really need is a model of optimum yield sustainable society futures.

Planning for survival would seem to have two faces, one being crisis avoidance and the other future creation. The focus of the first should be the development of contingency technologies, emergency preparedness programs and survival techniques geared to all possible forms of social disruption. The second face is the development of opportunity technologies, appropriate replacement technologies, transitional focused decentralization and diversity development. In both cases identification of vulnerability, targets and opportunity areas is essential.

We must also develop a dynamic inventory of capital stock, including estimates of life-times, costs and potential for replacement and improvement.

Finally, a major focus should be put on the continuity of social services — communication, information, education, recreation, health and civil protection. These are not only necessary conditions for survival but also tools for transition.

William Haddon Jr. in a brilliant article on the hazards of energy transfers of all kinds ("On The Escape of Tigers: An Ecologic Note", Technology Review, May 1970) cites ten strategies for reducing harmful interactions of energy, people and property. Only one of these is a pure strategy of prevention expressed by the concept "when in ignorance, refrain". The criteria for applying complete prevention is when the potential energy release is so large as to afford no meaningful resistance and the harmful effects are extremely costly in time and space. Then prevention alone becomes the exclusive strategy. We believe this strategy applies to both civil and military nuclear technologies. Despite the size of the threat in such technologies as large hydroelectric projects the impact in probability, in kind and amount of energy release and in terms of impact in space and time, would not warrant total prevention. It is for this reason that we argue for the total abandonment of nuclear power despite the realization that many of the strategies of limiting or restricting the possibility and effects of accidents have been applied. probability cannot override ethics in this case because the rate and magnitude problem and the intrinsic non-accountability of effects and costs under nuclear power are unethical, save as an exclusive option to survival. That is, as long as we have other options, we must say no to nuclear power. A corollary is that we cannot say never. But a further corrolary is that we must make every effort to keep our options open.

It must be emphasized that since the problem of nuclear

energy is not exclusively technical, but rather socio-technical, the solutions cannot be purely technical. Even a seemingly simple proposal to upgrade the existing inventory of housing to improve energy effectiveness and durability has powerful social and cultural barriers. Identification of these barriers and recommendations for their phased removal is also a key aspect of researching for survival. The major point is to seek a path of transition which is phased with the speed of change in the inventory of physical and attitudinal stock so that major dislocations and disruptions may be avoided. However, this transition will occur too slowly without catalysis and we must also research the catalysts that would be most effective. There are already mechanisms in place, for example, to move from "throw-away" goods to returnables and durables without threatening or allowing specific sectors of capital and labour to pay for the cost of such changes.

Besides the inventory of capital stock, we require a dynamic inventory of environmental goods and services and the potential for their enhanced use. In particular we ought to examine second law energy efficiencies in all the consuming sectors and attempt to maximize these by matching energy source to end use. By approaching the minimum work to achieve end uses we can vastly reduce energy consumption. This, of course, is radical to the point of appearing subversive, in that the electrical economy representing present policy is based on higher and higher levels of centralized power production and distribution with inevitably lower second law efficiencies. The use of waste and the re-use of goods are clearly at odds with the market economy as it now exists. Transfer to rental economies, cooperatives and barter economies will all be resisted by the status quo.

A Note on Personal and Social Freedom

WHILE THERE IS MERIT in President Carter's human rights interjection into international affairs it is so one-sided in content and application as to have a net offensiveness. It fails completely to distinguish between personal and social freedoms, and between deliberate and structural violence. Almost any communist country in the world offers the "freedoms from" to a greater extent than the U.S., that is they protect the social freedoms. It is true that this is sometimes at the expense of "freedom to" or the personal variety. But for vast numbers of people social security is the ultimate freedom. The pathetic lack of this security is in the U.S. where 26 million people are legally impoverished, i.e. have incomes below the minimum income. There may be twice this number who are literally impoverished spiritually and materially.

91

If we add to this poverty the huge inflation of psychosocial costs so dramatically illustrated by the mass looting on July 13, 1977, when the second impossible power failure occurred in New York City, it is clear that Mr. Carter's advisors do not have the sensitivity to understand hypocrisy or to recognize double standards and double dealings. It is correct for Mr. Carter to defend personal freedoms everywhere but he should apply his strictures to his allies as well as his enemies. But even more, he should understand the grotesque loss of freedom in the U.S. in the societal sense. Due process is a precious human social commodity, but freedom surely means more than due process in a social vacuum. Freedom must combine the traditional personal guarantees of human rights with the social freedom to live in dignity. Equality before the law is only half of freedom. Equality outside and after the law is the other necessary component to complete the victory of human freedom. It is not enough, and certainly not humanistic, to guarantee due process and all the other traditional personal freedoms to people disenfranchised and dispossessed by poverty. The coin freedom has two sides and both must be served.

Researching the Future

THE GENERAL VEHICLE for planning and implementing the political-economy of transition should be assigned to national policy institutes or institutes of urgent studies such as recommended by John Platt. We have earlier recommended an Institute of Relevant Studies (IRS).

While present reserves of oil, both for conventional and unconventional sources, will continue to be a significant resource they should be treated as capital for the future and managed for long-term availability. Their use for a variety of purposes will not be threatened.

With such a reduced availability of long-chain carbon molecules we must look again to renewables as a source for the various materials society requires which are now derived from petrochemicals. The return of chemurgy, or the use of agricultural products for chemical conversions particularly for developing countries, holds much promise. By securing raw materials for food, clothing, shelter and medicine, from local and regional agricultural sources, developing countries will be more self-sufficient nd induce lower environmental impacts. Coupling this with "agro-fermentation" processes for single cell protein and biomass and solar energy, these countries could theoretically extend their self-sufficiency to food and fuel. The destructive linkages of modern technology between food, fuel and fiber, involving the web of non-renewables and synthetics, could be broken in time. The other destructive linkages of copying Western industrialization and urbanization with its intrinsic anti-ecological elements of capital, technology and energy intensivity can also be broken. The new form of appropriate development can prevent the destruction of rural structures, indigenous cultures and traditions which are more in harmony with nature. In such a development the emergence of yet more nation-states based on market economics with heavy centralized institutions, high technology and large consumption rates can be hopefully avoided.

Bodies similar to John Platt's Institute of Urgent Studies but extended in scope to cover both disaster avoidance and future invention are what this author is proposing.

The major content of the Institute's work would be the following:

(1) Identification of major problems threatening survival;

(2) Setting priorities in terms of time and intensity to these threats;

(3) Developing solutions for these disaster-inducing problems;

(4) Integrating the above solutions into a comprehensive blueprint of a future designed to ensure life and fulfillment, i.e. inventing the future, involving the necessary restructuring of society and its sub-systems of politics, economics, culture and technology;

(5) Developing the policies and programs of an orderly transition from the present to the invented future, i.e. appropriate development;

(6) Active cooperation with the future assessment system.

We may define our "future assessment system" as comprising all those social groups and interested parties which are and should be concerned with anticipated, desirable and undesirable, changes social and technological, within the context of appropriate development. The binding of the elements of this system is the mutuality of concern for future developments. The pluralism is obvious in that multiple social tasks are involved in the processes that span assessment, forecasting of all kinds, the building of models and blueprints of the future and the policies and programs of transition. The diversity and interdisciplinarity arise from the connection that not only do we require the multiple visions of scientists, artists and mystics but the involvement of the non-academic, non-professional concerned citizen. The invented future will require high levels of social consensus. Consensus can only emerge from participation and understanding. And these goals in turn require the principles of openness, accessibility to information and acknowledgement of the right to know. The radical extension of the number of actors is a denial of elitism and an avowal of participatory values. Our inquiry system is a kind of People's Delphi, in recognition that not all oracles are expert or all experts oracles.

The major actors in our future assessment system are the proponents, their predictors, the people (and their predictors), the trade unions, and a special group, the invisible college of inquirers. These are an independent group of our most creative citizens of all disciplines and backgrounds. To identify people as a major actor is to acknowledge the emergence of a new class of social and environmental impacts which are intrinsically trans-boundary and often gobal. The immense burden of choice involved demands the search for consensus and higher levels of participation.

The Politics of Grass Roots

A CITIZEN'S MOVEMENT for survival must now seriously create viable alternatives for our economic, political and value systems. They must translate these into a political movement that is issue-oriented and which seeks a constituency which cuts across traditional party lines. Alas, we do not have a successful historical model by which to guide our efforts; our complex of goals is new and our constituency not predetermined. Nevertheless the politics of transition will require the organized efforts of a new constituency.

What seems necessary is that the environmental movement plus its allies among the public and in all parties must seek an effective basis for lobbying and even for the seeking and accepting of political responsibility. We must seek a political base, at the municipal level, that is most accessible to independents. People power can best be realized at this level due to the prohibitive cost of politics at the provincial or federal level. The environmental movement must seek a power base in munipal politics across the country. This is the ecology of grass-roots. This broad citizens coalition can now expect more official support and sanction as the recognition of the irreoncilable dualities of formal politics operating within the system spreads. We have passed from policies in search of government to governments in search of policies. The politics of fashion which first absorbed the environmental issue is being converted by reality to a new fashion in politics.

There are two major organizational steps to be taken in the evolution of the politics of grass-roots. The first is the establishment of municipal, metropolitan and regional survival councils. These councils will be composed of the existing national and local groups concerned with major issues of environment, population, energy, war, etc., as well as local issues of development. An adequate information support system will be necessary, derived from independent scientists and engineers who share the concerns. The next stage is to link the local and regional councils into a national body which can take up issues that are national and international. A national organization of non-governmental organizations or NGO's can be a powerful voice and lobby for meaningful social change. The task is to create multiple non-hierarchal decentralized but coordinated networks. The art of social networks must be mastered if we are going to communicate effectively among the various members of the new lobby.

The conditions in this country and the world are now ripe for the development of this kind of political strategy. Each city and region should explore the possibility of an establishing municipal survival councils, using existing groups and natural allies from the church to the trade unions. These councils could then be the launching platform for political action. Hopefully these groups could lead to the flowering of the politics of grass-roots. For the first time in history we need a politics that denies political power but affirms the power of values.

The example of New Zealand in evolving a politics of grass-roots is worth examining. New Zealand was the first to create a Values Party, the only party to consistently combine the twin goals of equity and environment. Now the "green tide" as it has been called is sweeping far abroad. In France the Mouvement Ecologie is its extension. It has now become clear that traditional ideologies from left to right are corrupted by power and subverted by the system, sharing as they do an ideology of progress and a worship of technology. There are many people who now operate under the flag of these traditional political parties but whose loyalties are dedicated to the resolution of fundamental problems. It is perhaps time to translate the ecology of grass-roots into the political form of a Canadian Values Party, hopefully enlisting all those in every party who share a common cause. Saskatchewan, for many reasons, might be the most appropriate region for such an intiative. The catalysts may already have begun to work. A broad coalition cutting across all political lines has emerged around the issue of the proposed extension of uranium mining. Moreover Saskatchewan has multiple political traditions embracing principles of social responsibility which could increase the fertility for the birth of a new constituency and a new politics.

A penetrating analysis on the qualitatively novel grass roots movement that is presently surfacing on a global level has been noted by Hine and Gerlack. Virginia Hine, University of Miami anthropologist and Luther P. Gerlack of the University of Minnesota have observed a new structural form and mode of functioning among "movement networks" which they term a "segmented polycephalous network" and designated by the acronym SP(I)N. This is hideous academic jargon but the analysis is interesting. A SP(I)N is a multiple, non-hierarchal, non-elitist, decentralized network, often linked by a focused alliance of groups with overlapping memberships. SP(I)N's provide a kind of deliberate organization segmentation (hydra-headed) which allows powerlessness to be levered into power without curruption. Integration is eschewed through a powerful consensus of basic values within the spin, but an equally powerful diversity and even controlled conflict by the differing segments which prevents consolidation and take-over and eludes bureaucratization. Models are Clamshell, Crabshell and Abalone Alliances in the U.S., these having the additional and necessary virtue of being non-violent on principle. The gobal anti-nuclear movement is evolving into a SP(I)N. The form of emergence of a Canadian Values Party could well be designated by SP(I)N.

The Search for Community
WE SHOULD NOT MERELY search for the lost community because it is becoming fashionable but because the community is a survival unit of social existence. The new concept of community will be radically different than those of the past in that we will have open communities, not just physically open but with real connections to all communities, mainly through the use of electronic networking. We may define a community as a network of mutuality even "mutual coercion by mutual consent". It is a self-sustaining social unit connected by "a system of mutual obligations, of mutual assessments and of mutual links" (Gordon Rattray Taylor).

The size of community depends on the definition. Gordon Rattray Taylor believes a community or "assessment group" as he calls it, cannot be larger than 1200, in order to comply with the notion that every member can make a personal assessment of every other member, i.e. every member can retain individual identity within the total web of social and personal relationships. Such a community is like a large or extended family in that inter-assessment allows us to accept each member entirely for what he or she is becoming. Attachment and belonging, both to the physical environment and to each other, creates emotional links and investments to place and people. Cooperation is the norm not the deviation. In effect the "tragedy of the commons" is overcome by mutual obligations. The community also permits and catalyzes participation. In effect the community is a participatory political unit.

There are several problems with this concept. In the past communities have themselves become stabilized and inbred. They have exerted pressures on the novel spirit to conform to more narrow visions which pervade. They have stifled the voyages of the mind by collective social prying and praying. To a large degree these negative aspects derive from isolation and small minds. We are thinking much more of globalized villages or inter-connected communities where dynamic exchanges of people and ideas are fostered. The community is not so much bounded by separation as by its own internal bonds. A large city is thus a great number of such communities filled into a larger network. The city would become a cluster of communities. But within each community there are mutualized activities of production, consumption, recreation and education. They are self-sufficient to a very high degree and based as far as possible on ecological principles, i.e. they are social ecosystems. These are essentially organic social units in that the atoms of sociological structure, i.e. norms, roles, goals, status, reward, etc., are functional, integrated, socially useful, non-hierarchical and retain the distinction of individual identity and differentiation. We will certainly have hierarchy, but it will be horizontal hierarchy; not elitist and not based on power leverage. In the end there is strength in small numbers.

Community tends to create the psycho-social phase of evolution in that what is handed down from generation to generation is more intact, less diffused and hopefully less homogenized. The emotional network cements the entire process so that children of children inherit a love for their friend's parents and their parent's friends. The homogenized mass culture of modern society should give way to great diversity as each community innovates in its own novel fashion. Personalization is reinstituted in community life and barter will tend to replace money. Marx's cash nexus is overcome as transactions become direct and personal. McLuhan's "learning a living" becomes realizable.

Up until now community has been restored by counter-culture activities — by the opting out or dropping out process. This type of "greening of America" is too slow for the pace of adverse change. However, the task of accelerating and planning the creation of community is enormous if not impossible.

Mass culture suffers from two terrible costly distortions of the human psyche. These are anomie or anomia and closure. Anomie is the state of alienation, the sense of meaningless and incapacity to cope, which leads to motivationless violence, to others or to oneself, i.e. homicide, suicide or even genocide. We can see the rising costs of social pathology and yet manage to obscure them in our accounting systems. Two diseases — cancer and anomia — are the plagues of progress and are exacting a fighteningly large toll from society, still unpaid but coming due. Both are technological diseases directly and indirectly. Both are the result of the malnutrition of affluence.

Closure is the most subtle impoverishment of the mind whereby in growing from children to adults in a mass society with an adaptive monoculture we close off debate within ourselves. We place ideas in isolated confinement. We permanently lose our sense of wonder and connection. Closure is the ultimate state on non-involvement. We allow others, preferably status persons, to choose for us at every level of our life from work to politics. Closure and anomia lead to the loss of personal autonomy so necessary for survival. These are fed by a huge monoculture and nourished by hierarchal politics. Contributing factors are crowding and poverty permitted by the technology of the built environment in a system of recognized exploitation.

Appropriate Development
THE CORE OF our program must reflect the priority and urgency of the global problems. Since we have argued that maldistribution as an operational issue is the most critical, the major thrust of our program must be to solve the problem of global inequity. This involves radically new concepts of international relations, and, in particular, a new mode of international development. Canadian initiatives toward solutions will have to concentrate on how to transfer appropriate development to the nations and peoples now suffering inequities.

We must begin by affirming as undeniable that a certain threshold of economic development is required by all societies to provide for their real needs of survival and fulfillment. We must equally affirm that the profilgate production and consumption patterns of the economically developed countries is wasteful and in itself a source of major environmental psychological and resource disruption. To achieve the former condition is to pass through a stage of necessary economic development. To eschew the latter is to accelerate the ecocide of the planet. We must therefore affirm the need for the developing world to complete their development in order to make it consistent with regional, national and global survival. But we equally affirm that such completion should not be an imitation of the West. At the same time we must attend to the necessary changes in the direction of Canadian development for the sake of the same consistency. A critical priority of Canada is to help define an appropriate form of development for the world and to develop plans and policies for its achievement.

Appropriate development is composed of a set of internal and external policies and programs. Both of these sets of policies will be guided by the unique cultural, geographical and geopolitical conditions for each particular region. But without international and reciprocal programs with other parts of the world it would be difficult if not impossible to achieve the goals.

The three main elements of these "external" programs are aid, trade and technology transfer. While there is a certain overlap in these concepts, their general definition is as follows. Aid is a recognition of global interdependence in the common interest of survival. It is not a gift of charity. Aid should be the anonymous transfer of surpluses of goods and services from global banks operated by the U.N. to those countries suffering temporary or critical deficiencies. Aid should be unconditional, non-repayable, and international. Aid should be supplied without influence and without strings. It may be goods, capital or services and its nature should be determined by the recipient nation. Much of the development of these concepts should be done in the Institute of Relevant Studies (IRS).

Canada should take the initiative for the establishment of a group of world banks administered by the U.N. These could begin with four basic banks — food, capital, information and technical. The latter three should be conceived within the context of appropriate development.

Trade, unlike aid, is the continuous exchange of goods and services on the basis of acceptable mutual rewards and needs between the trading partners. Trade is not purely economic but should involve, like aid, the building of a visible interdependence designed to optimize global security and survival. Canadian initiatives here should concentrate on the search for meaningful trade with Third World countries rather than the usual division of spoils among the Have-Nations. Perhaps the nearest view of our development model is described in the series of essays "Another Development" edited by Max Nerfin of the Dag Hammerskjold Foundation (1977) which is described as "need oriented, endogenous, self-reliant, ecologically sound and based on structural transformations."

The traditional instrument of development is technology transfer and capital. The instrument for appropriate development is appropriate technology. It is here that it is possible for major Canadian initiatives. The Brace Institute at McGill and John Todd's New Alchemists in Prince Edward Island are world leaders in this area.

Appropriate technology has five major aspects

1. It is socially appropriate;

2. It is culturally appropriate;
3. It is environmentally appropriate;
4. It is thermodynamically appropriate;
5. It is humanly appropriate.

Appropriate technology and development will emphasize self-reliance but not to the exclusion of interdependence. Emphasis on indigenous material and human resources will be a natural consequence. Scale will be a variable in technology adjusting itself to optimizing economic benefits and vulnerability avoidance and the high costs of transportation and distribution. This will also be true of the level of decentralization. Within decentralized communities, centralized supply, distribution, re-cycling and re-use will be sought for their economies and efficiencies.

Appropriate technology like appropriate development will exhibit high levels of diversity and decentralization in order to minimize vlunerability to major disruptions and their accompanying social costs. By definition appropriateness is modified by the total environment and their specific starting conditions. Thus appropriate development would be highly differentiated regionally. It would not ipso facto preclude growth but such growth would always be organic and intimately related to the continued availability of life support. It would tend to evolve to a "stable state" as limits became inevitable and necessary.

Despite this differentiation there could be two or three broad general models of appropriate development, correlated with the specific starting conditions and the communality of demographic, geological, geographical and development factors. A Canadian model of appropriate development could thus have a high degree of relevancy for countries such as Australia and the U.S. and to a lesser degree with Sweden, Norway and New Zealand. On the other hand, the principles are universal, thus Canada should also begin to develop a set of models designed for specific regions at various stages of development and with widely different physical and human environments.

Ultimately the entire spectrum of Canadian initiatives for survival could best be accomplished by a new agency, an Institute for Urgent Studies. In the meantime it might be possible for existing institutions to begin these tasks. Such agencies and groups as the Economic Council of Canada, Science Council of Canada, the Office of Energy Conservation, the Centre for Advanced Concepts, and the International Development Agency could start. But encouragement and support from the survival councils will be a necessary aspect for the realization of these initiatives. We should immediately assign specific authorities and priorities to these existing government agencies. For example, our Economic Council should be researching a viable spaceship economic model based on steady-state consumption through resource management, conservation and recycling. Economics as a discipline seems little inclined to such a task, yet it must be done. An accurate cost effectiveness analysis of pollution might well prove false the economics of unlimited growth.

Our Science Council should initiate and support the technology required to solve both internally and externally the urgent problems of the quadrilemma. Our International Development Centre should examine the means of overcoming the world maldistribution problem and of identifying the kinds of foreign aid required. They should be researching survival foods such as high protein "universal and complete foods" (UCF) made from wheat protein. We need an active national Environmental Council to create a national program of ecological sanity. It should adopt, as should all government agencies, the principle of public hearings and independent participation. Information Canada should disseminate information "Swedish style" by acknowledging the right of the public to know and to participate in the great decisions now required. Not only conceptual development but implementation could be coordinated by the new institute proposed, IRS.

A highly specific program which Canada is ideally suited to initiate is an International Protein and Food Bank. This organization would stockpile protein and other foods supplied by the have-countries to be withdrawn by countries in crisis conditions. A national contribution in the case of portein would be the development of a universal and complete food, designated as the Canadian Peace Biscuit based on wheat protein with an adjusted amino acid profile and capable of being stockpiled with long shelf-life. Other countries with excess protein and food sources should be encouraged to join with us in these proposals and developments.

Of all technologies and developments energy is the single most significant in shaping the future. Thus energy policy is a most critical element in the transition to sustainability.

Chapter 6

Energy and the Sustainable Society

ENERGY IS highly correlated with both the quantity and quality of life. The good news is that a certain lower threshold of energy is necessary for life-support to supply the goods and services necessary for survival. The bad news is that a higher threshold of consumption threatens the delivery and availability of environmental goods and services, thus threatening survival. The ideal energy policy is to steer a course between limits, i.e. at consumption levels which optimize the quantity-quality mix.

At the same time energy production and consumption is also highly correlated to the nature of economic and political institutions, as well as values and life-styles. The corruptibility of power is at once physical and political. The resolution of conflicts between too little and too much lies in matching energy technologies and social institutions in such a way as to conform to ecological principles whose design is survival and stability. And, of course, we must subscribe simultaneously to environment and equity for both are essential to survival.

Throughout the Western industrialized world energy policy stands centre-stage in the concern for the future. Since energy is ultimately the measure of all things, energy policy represents options of the future, determining to a great extent our politics, economics, culture and lifestyle. Historical growth rate policies based on unlimited visions of cheap oil and gas are rapidly collapsing. But growth addiction remains rampant particularly in the case of utilities who have simply shifted their techno-logical strategy to nuclear power. This continued planning for high historical growth seems independent of country or ideology. There is a bare tokenism towards conservation. On the other hand most Western governments are breaking with this pattern and have gone beyond the fashionable to promote and implement genuine conservation policies. The debate on supply, demand and the desirability of particular technologies has now been joined in these countries.

The Federal Picture

FOLLOWING THE 1973-74 oil crisis, members of OECD's International Energy Agency agreed in part to implement conservation programs, particularly related to oil. IAE's first published report was summarized in the OECD Observer of September/October, 1976, No. 83. Clearly, the Canadian record in an overall sense s of that date was one of the worst.

Taking taxes on gasoline as a percent of price only, only the U.S., New Zealand and Japan had lower increases. Fourteen countries had percent increases well above 50%. Canada's was less than 40%. In 1975 Canada's reduction in consumption over pre-energy-crisis projections was exceeded by 13 countries, including the U.S., Belgium, Japan and the Netherlands. All of the latter had reduced consumption by about 20%, almost twice Canada's reduction. Even more revealing was that 15 countries exceeded Canada in their reduction of total energy requirements (primary) per unit of gross domestic product between 1973 and 1975.

In terms of pricing of oil products Canada had the second cheapest gasoline cost of member countries and the lowest heating oil and heavy fuel costs of all 17 countries (as of December 31, 1975). In terms of *real* consumer prices of gasoline and fuel oils Canada had the lowest prices based on 1973 fuel prices.

An excellent indicator of serious conservation programs is the direct fuel cost of auto transportation (energy/passenger-mile). The Canadian ratio was the *highest* of all member countries by a significant amount, ranging from 3 to 2 times as large as most, even 50% higher than the U.S.!

In terms of industry efficiency covering energy consumption per ton of six industrial products, Canada was the second highest for crude steel and pulp and paper and by far the highest for petroleum products, i.e. twice as high as the U.S. It was also one of the highest for wet process cement.

While there are indications that Canadian policy in regard to conservation is improving it may well by a typical "too little — too late" adjustment. The Office of Energy Conservation, EMR, is certainly an excellent development but when one considers that EMR employs 2000 persons only 35 of which are in OEC as of 1977 one could conclude that our government has not "put their

ENERGY AND THE SUSTAINABLE SOCIETY

money where their mouth is". However more recent developments indicate policies directed to increased commitments to conservation.

On July 4, 1978, Energy Minister Alistair Gillespie announced Ottawa's plans to pump $380 million into renewable energy in the next five years, a truly substantial increase over the meagre expenditures in the past, ($14 million earmarked for 1978-79). So far only $6 million has been actually assigned. But is this really putting their money where their mouth is or mouthing policy which will never be implemented? Is this the politics of election year, a response to the PC's promise of $400 million over 12 years? Is there a solar-operated bandwagon in Canada? At the same time the provinces have begun to move. Ontario may build 17 small hydro dams to be traded off against increased conventional expansion. This only totals a peak of 1600 megawatts and a base of 500 so it hardly replaces one nuclear plant. The smell of tokenism is again discernible. A Quebec crown corporation has also developed a renewables program to replace petroleum dependency by about half by 1990. Together with a conservation program Energy Minister Guy Joron hopes to cut per capita consumption from 3.5% to 0.3% by 1990, a truly impressive goal. But he has to defeat the most powerful institution in the province, Hydro Quebec, to translate policy into implementation.

Meanwhile many studies indicate feasibility to biomass particularly methanol from energy plantations, e.g. poplar trees or from a variety of organic wastes and the direct combustion of such wastes.

Despite this promising beginning, skepticism should guide our actions. Mr. Gillespie's energy policy of allowing "a thousand flowers to bloom", like Mao's, will fail as capital shortages demand priority. Already this has led to the cancellation of the La Prade heavy water plant in Gentilly, Quebec, after millions had been spent. Nuclear slow-down and bad planning has created a glut of heavy water for this virtually exclusive Ontario development. Thus federal spending will have to choose between pipelines, synthetic crude, nuclear, hydro and renewables/conservation. It is likely the latter will suffer the first cuts.

The vulnerability of the Canadian non-renewable resource base is hardly questioned anymore particularly in view of the pressures from the U.S. for accessibility, and the response to those pressures from those who profit from export. Nevertheless its implications are misunderstood, or denied. Not only in Canada but in the U.S., estimates by industry of oil and gas reserves have been seriously overestimated. In the case of Canada this over-estimation has been tragic and it has led to a travesty of policy. Professor Ken North of Carleton University has been the most consistent, and unfortunately ignored, prophet of our fossil fuel reserves. Given the U.S.'s voracious appetite for oil and gas, all our reserves, proven and potential, would contribute only a few years' extension to their life-time reserves.

Even our tar sands, of which about 5% represents recoverable amounts by available technology, would only extend the total North American reserve life for four years. By 1984 the U.S. will have an oil deficit of 10 million barrels per day (b/d) while Canada itself will have a deficit of 1.5 million b/d, almost equivalent to our total production in 1975. The growing deficits are the consequence of the growth in consumption Canada would need to discover and develop in very rapid order 15 fields the size of Leduc (80,000 b/d) and all in the same basin. The cost of exploration, production and delivery would be enormous while the entire discoveries would feed North America's consumption for only one year. Only massive conservation leading to large decreases in consumption could offset the growth in deficits. The European Economic Community feels this huge burden of oil imports feeds the economic problems of the West. It is critical that we reduce negative balance of payments. The Economic Summit Conference in July 1978 considered that reduced oil consumption was critical.

In the case of natural gas Canada is equally vulnerable. By 1985 increased and new demand will mean that exploitation of the capacity of all existing fields will still lead to a shortfall of 0.5 billion barrels per year. None of the pipeline proposals solve either the U.S.'s or Canada's growing gas requirements but only serve to deepen the crisis of shortfall after a few years. This is the classical exponential growth trap of the supply-demand dilemma and applies equally to highways and autos as it does to pipelines and fossil fuels. Yet Canada is pursuing the futile and counter-productive search for more oil and gas instead of attending to the real problem of shifting our energy dependency in type and quantity to energy income sources. The only other long-term alternatives are fission breeders and coal, neglecting *in situ* technologies for oil sands and shales. Breeders and these *in situ* technologies are either not available and in the case of the breeders are questionable sources from many points of view. Nuclear power in any case supplies baseload electricity and does not solve the problem of liquid fuel requirements, the two not being substitutable. Cars run on gasoline not electricity. It is inescapable that coal, despite its difficult distribution and pollution problems, must be viewed as a serious bridging fuel in the transition period.

In Canada the major energy-producing and energy-using industries consume over 50% of our national energy. But they produce only about 10% of national employment. Most of our employment is in the merchandising and service industries. Yet Canadian corporate and government postures continue to sell the myth of energy as the source of jobs and economic viability. The fact is that West Germany, Sweden and Switzerland have higher GNP/capital than we do, have less unemployment and about half the energy per capita. A country like New Zealand has virtually no unemployment, a GNP per capita about two-thirds of ours and an energy consumption per capita 20% of ours.

Two major reports — The Ford Foundation's Energy Policy and that of the Oak Ridge Institute for Energy Analysis have both concluded that the U.S. could reduce energy growth to between 1.5% and 2% per year for the next 20 to 30 years while still experiencing a real GNP growth of about twice this rate. Canada is better off in its energy reserves and more wasteful that the U.S. A growth of 1.5% in energy to the year 2010 is highly feasible with real GNP growth of at least 3% per year. The myth of direct proportionality between energy use and economic growth has been dispelled and, in any case, it is uncertain which is the independent variable. The fact is that there is much variation between countries. Bruce Hannon's computations would indicate that for each 10^{15} Btu (Quad) of thermal or nuclear electricity our society produces we will lose 75,000 jobs over our entire economy, a further negative feature of increasing generating capacity.

The problem of "peaking", i.e. of having peak loads on capital stock, whether energy supply systems or public buildings, is a serious obstacle to the management of resource demand. In the case of electrical supply systems it means we require an "excess" supply to serve peak demands for something of the order of 10 to 15% of total time. Work peaks in one 8-hour segment mean that all services must be geared to that period while they may virtually be idle for two thirds of the time. This is true of transit, schools, office buildings and a borad variety of services. We also have leisure and life-style peaks which again cluster demand over roughly 20 to 25% of time. De-peaking or "smoothing out" demand could reduce the need for future supply by perhaps 25%. However, utilities, public or private, socialist or capitalist, tend to be universally supply (growth) oriented and have intrinsic internal and external mandates to expand supply rather than managing demand. This orientation is built into the rate structure by encouraging use or by having a fixed return rate on consumption, i.e. the larger the consumption, the larger the profit.

In the "built environment," peaking in the use of public building is particularly wasteful. Commercial buildings are closed over 50% of the time and recreational and entertainment facilities may be used even less. Investigation of techniques to maximize the use of public buildings or even public transit such as subways at off-peak times could lead to significant savings. "Metro-education" was such an idea developed by a Montreal town planner.

Wasted energy is literally wasted jobs. Throw-away products are throw-away jobs. Thus comparing fossil fuel production and utilities which require over $100,000 investment per job to servces ($9,500), apparel ($5,000), textiles, wholesale and retail trade (about $10,000), food (about $18,000), and all manufacturing (about $19,000 on the average), we can see which kind of investment generates jobs. An investment of one million dollars in service industries will generate 10 times the jobs of energy industries.

There is a curious irony that Canada, one of the richest countries in the world, currently has one of the highest unemployment rates since World War II (real unemployment could easily be as high as 10%, with certain regions even higher). As many as 5 million people live at or near the "poverty line". We are still suffering an uncontrollable rate of inflation and yet we are told that the answer is greater energy consumption. How is it that we are consuming more energy per capita than ever before and at the same time our economic woes are at their most serious stage. To continue to correlate in our simplistic manner energy consumption with GNP is no longer even conventional wisdom. It is true that *total* employment has increased but this is not because of increased energy consumption. On the contrary, enhanced use of energy decreases empoyment. Only the actual increase in goods and services has led to increased employment.

In Canada the largest industries while contributing significantly to GNP do not enhance employment. On the contrary, they are the largest energy consumers. The increase of productivity or output per worker has invariably been accompanied by a decrease (proportionally) in the percent employment of that industry. This is also true of agriculture. Fifty years ago agriculture required 10 times the person hours. Utilities and other energy producing industries, aside from the construction period, have had small employment increases relative to their outputs and revenues. Bruce Hannon of Illinois' Centre for Advanced Computation has calculated that for each consumer dollar spent on electricity 502,473 Btu of fossil fuels were required while the labour units per dollar are o.044. Comparing this for example to furniture manufacture it is 1/15 as energy intensive and twice as labour intensive. Women's and children's clothing is over twice as labour intensive and requires only 33,065 Btu per dollar.

Second Law Efficiency

ONE OF THE most compelling and significant concept is that of Second Law Efficiency (SLE). Simply expressed it deals with the efficiency with which heat or chemical or nuclear energy from fuels are exchanged with work. For a particular energy end-use there is a necessary associated theoretical work. Second Law Efficiency is the ratio of the actual work expended to this theoretical work required. A second significant aspect of SLE is that by matching what we call the grade or quality of the energy used to accomplish the desired end to the nature of the requirement we can maximize SLE. This may be understood symbolically in that it would be inappropriate to use a silk embroidered blouse to clean an oven nor a diesel engine to run a calculator.

The grade of energy is measured by the temperature of the heat system in the conversion from heat to work. Thus many industrial processes such as smelting require high grade energy, that is they operate at very high temperatures. The moving of large masses through the use of motors whether combustion or electrical types are other examples of high grade energy.

What is of interest is that almost one half of the entire energy consumption in Canada is low-grade that is low temperature heat as in space, and water heating and low temperature industrial requirements. Electricity on the other hand, is a form of high-grade energy. Only 12% of our total end-use of energy is obligatory electricity as in electro-chemical metallurgical processes, electric communications of all kinds and electric railways. Even if we included electric motors the total electrical end-use is only 18%. It incredibly inappropriate and inefficient to generate energy thermally or through nuclear fission at temperatures of thousands of degrees and with over two thirds wasted for end-uses such as space and water heating requiring temperature ranges of 100 to 200°F.

Many normal activities in our society have SLE's of less that 10%, i.e. residential and commercial space heating: 6%; residential and commercial water heating: 3%; air conditioning and refrigeration: 5%; automobile propulsion: 10%; petroleum refining: 9%; cement manufacture: 10%; paper production: less than 1%; etc. The average SLE in the U.S. derived by weighing the amount of fuel used for the various purposes is only 8.3%. The implication is that *very large amounts* of energy can be saved by achieving very high second law efficiencies. Theoretically if we could achieve an average SLE of 75% in our total energy system we could save over 65% of the fuel energy presently used. This is a very large quantity. Based on our 1975 use of fuels this saving represents about 6.5 Quads (a quad is 10^{15} British thermal units or Btu). This is equivalent to 3 million barrels of petroleum per day.

The Ontario Situation

MANY OF THE arguments presented here would also apply to Ontario as well. It is true that Ontario is the most vulnerable region in Canada respecting energy. On the other hand Ontario is the largest and most wasteful energy consumer. Thus the potential for conservation is very large.

When one considers that Ontario is planning to spend some $40 billion by 2000 on a nuclear program we can certainly see the wisdom of abandoning this extravagant, expensive and counter-productive program. Energy Probe has estimated that an $11 billion investment in conservation and renewables in Ontario will save $11 billion and relieve all further nuclear expansion to 1995. This would involve providing solar space heating to 500,000 dwellings (about 45% of total).

There is little question that Quebec, Ontario and Canada as a whole have the luxury to defer any further nuclear growth until at least 2000.

The Maritimes

NOVA SCOTIA CAN certainly expand coal production. New Brunswick has learned the costly lesson of nuclear power with huge overruns of its first CANDU. Moreover since equal baseload generation is usually required as back-up New Brunswick will have far more power than it requires and is now scrounging for customers.

Prince Edward Island under the guidance of its premier, Alex Campbell, is seriously examining the prospect of a sustainable society. It is no accident that Dr. Todd, founder of the New Alchemists, an ecological group, has constructed his remarkable self-sustaining habitat, the Ark, in Prince Edward Island or that P.E.I. has resisted joining the CANDU club.

The Quebec Situation

VIEWED AS A disaggregated but not necessarily independent entity, an almost ideal energy policy for Quebec combines a strong conservation program with a major commitment to renewable energy sources. The reason for this assertion is multifold. In the first place, Quebec still has some unused 25,000 MW of electrical power from hydro sources including James Bay, plus other potential sources. Even at an extravagant anticipated demand of 5% per year this will suffice beyond the year 2000. The fact that Hydro-Quebec correctly characterized by Energy Minister Joron as a "state within a state" and by former Minister Cournoyer as "the larger of the two", is still projecting demand at the grotesque and irresponsible growth rate of 8%. This only reinforces the view that this growth addicted public utility with its mania for corruptible power must be made responsible to people, to government and to Nature.

Three policies essential for the preservation of Quebec's unique culture (not necessarily separatism) are job creation, support for small business and maintaining an agricultural community. Conservation and renewable energy sources are highly conducive to achieving all three of these policies. These issues exist outside politics because this vision of Quebec could be as desirable inside or outside of confederation. We believe this ultimately should be the policy of Canada as a whole, but regionally it applies best to Quebec, the Maritimes and to a degree the middle Western provinces.

The Oregon experiment with total returnables rather than disposable containers indicates that retrnables do not impede the viability of the beverage and food industries. In Oregon returnables have increased employment and have proven intrinsically more labour intensive.

An energy policy based on maximizing conservation and renewable energy sources accomplishes the optimization of social, economic and environmental goals. Some of the major advantages of this policy are:

(1) It slows down the required rate of capital formation for high technology development and is therefore anti-inflationary. Canadian investment in oil and gas exploration alone has been estimated at $180 billion. Investment in nuclear power plants could be as high as $100 billion by the year 2000. Hydro-Quebec alone is seeking sanction to build 35 nuclear plants before the end of the millenium.

(2) The reduction in the rate of capital formation allows for greater flexibility and balance in the allocation of capital to social, economic and environmental goals. Since bad energy tends to drive out good, this translates into significant reductions in demand equal to the planned increases in supply. The difference in this invested capital can be applied to the development and maintenance of human resources, i.e. to health, education and an improved quality of life. The latter is actually an intrinsic side benefit of reduced production and consumption.

(3) Since the cost of energy supply and conversion is significantly larger than the cost of conservation, there are real capital savings in conserving energy. However, added to

economic advantages are savings in unpaid or deferred social and environmental costs associated with supply. Conservation is not only resource but environmental management. According to the Office of Energy Conservation at an estimated cost of $6.3 billion we could retrofit the total residential sector with optimum insulation. This results in a cost of 50 cents per million Btu. Comparing this to the cost of delivered energy the figures are $5 for gas and $10 for nuclear power per million Btu. The pay-back time is less than 10 years with a total useful life of 20 years. Total energy savings in that time amount to 60 Quad (6 quadrillion or 6×10^{15} Btu or over 80% of our total energy consumption in 1976 at a minimum value of $10 billion (1975). ($0.5b/year).

Using calculations of the American Institute of Architects (published in 1972) we could save the equivalent of 1.25 million barrels per day of petroleum just by employing energy-efficient systems in old and new buildings. This is equivalent to investing some $50 billion by 1990 to provide that amount of petroleum and would cost consumers about $100 billion to purchase.

Of particular interest is the possibility of using waste industrial steam to produce electricity (cogeneration). This is a very common practice in Sweden and West Germany. The potential for this in Canada could amount to an equivalent of about 60,000 barrels of oil per day by 1980. By 1985 it could save the equivalent of 5000 MW(e) nuclear (at half the price of electricity) according to a study by the Dow Chemical Company for the National Science Foundation in June 1975. Perhaps as much as 35% of industry's total energy use is in the form of process steam. Thus cogeneration could lead to huge savings. Energy consumption retrofits in commercial buildings have led to a 60% decrease in steam use and a 30% decrease in electrical use at the Hermann Building, M.I.T.

A particularly ambitious study by the Bonneville Power Administration of Portland, Oregon in 1976 reviewed a broad variety of reports and examples of conservation world-wide. The net result of this study indicates that savings of between 30 and 40% are feasible in all consuming sectors and that "high impact conservation programs create more jobs than would be created by building new power plants to generate an equivalent amount of energy." This conclusion is borne out by studies by the Federal Energy Administration, the State of Colorado and the Senate Commerce Committee staff in the U.S.

(4) Conservation and particularly renewable energy sources are labour rather than energy or capital intensive and thus are excellent generators of jobs and reduce inflation. It has been estimated by various groups, i.e. ERDA, OEC, Science Council, etc.

that conservation investment is approximately 50% labour intensive. Thus the national retrofit program would create 200,000 person-years of employment. The $2 billion Ontario Hydro is planning to invest in the Darlington nuclear complex will create 70,000 person-years of employment. An equal amount invested in conservation will yield 125,000 person-years of employment. It has also been estimated that investment in solar technologies yields 2.5 times the jobs that nuclear power plants generate. Moreover these jobs are varied, more dispersed and much more amenable to small business ventures than nuclear projects. We need not confine ourselves to solar space/water heating. ERDA has estimated that photovoltaics will cost $500 per peak KW in 1986, compared to over $1000 for nuclear. With a government-owned industry producing silicon cells, costs could be reduced by as much as 50%.

Just three major conservation measures in the residential area, i.e. insulation, automatic thermostats and proper caulking and weatherizing would create about 50,000 jobs for each $200 million invested. Moreover, the jobs created tend to be localized in urban or near urban centres and to be moderately skilled, thus avoiding the problems of importing transient workers for "boom town" expensive energy-intensive projects with their high social costs and disruptive impact. Large centralized energy projects tend to yield maximum employment in the construction period and then only to construction workers. These workers are protected by solar technologies but many other types of small businesses are also supported.

It is interesting that both the Sheet Metal and Air Conditioning Contractors' Association and the Sheet Metal Workers' International Association agree that solar is very labour intensive. It can create about 3 times as many jobs as can nuclear power. Retrofitting 5 million homes in Canada to obtain 50% of their space/water heating from solar devices would create 25 million hours of work per year for 10 years. Moreover, the job mix is desirable, with far more skilled tradespersons being used instead of professional technically trained people, i.e. 9 to 1 compared to 2 to 1 for nuclear.

(5) Not only do these policies generate new jobs but they create a broader distribution of jobs by type and location. This tends to overcome disparities or discontinuities in job creation, characteristic of huge centralized high technology energy projects.

(6) An ancillary advantage deriving from labour intensivity and decentralization is that it affords great opportunities to small business, indigenous business and community enterprises. These, in turn, when applied to conservation and renewable

business reinforce all the other advantages accruing to these policies.

John F. Bulloch, President of the Canadian Federation of Independent Businesses gave credence to the above proposition when he stated "Nuclear power means high capacity, centralized generating stations surrounded by a technocracy and armed guards. Control will be in the hands of either big government or large oligopolies. Nuclear power, in other words, is synonymous with a philosophy of concentration of power. Solar power, on the other hand, is ideally suited for deconcentration of population and growth of smaller communities. Because each home or community would have in effect its own generating station, solar-powered homes and communities can be located almost anywhere without concern for loss of power in transmission. And the manufacture, installation and servicing of these solar power systems would provide work for tens of thousands of small firms. This is one industry that should be Canadian-owned and controlled."

On the other hand components and engineering for nuclear power plants are supplied by very large firms, many of them multinationals. Even in the CANDU system between 20 and 25% of the components materials and skills are imported.

(7) The combined policy of conservation and renewables buys time, allowing us to apply our energy research and development program to the solution of technical barriers, such as the more complete utilization of renewable energy technologies, including solar power generation. There is ample evidence that the "learning curve" for solar technologies yields short to medium term estimates of feasibility including electrical generation. Combining significant increases in the efficiency of silicon cells with dramatic reductions in electrical demand, i.e. achieved by solar space/water heating and cooling, improved coefficients of performance of electric gadgets, etc. and matching source with end-use there is every reason to believe that a solar electric power system could make significant contributions in the next 25 to 50 years. If we examine the broad array of electric devices we now purchase, from air conditioners to washing machines the range of power consumption is almost 100%. For relatively small additional investments life-time efficiency is radically improved, often at a rate of payback of less than one year.

Waste heat recuperators for high-temperature furnaces can lead to fuel savings of 25%. According to Widmer and Gyftopoulos of Nuclear Engineering, M.I.T., $1.5 billion annually invested in these recuperators could save $6 billion in fuel in the U.S. Incidentally, these two authors (Technology Review, June 1977, p. 32), admit that nuclear electricity will cost 50% more than coal generated for every new annual quad (10^{15} Btu) of production, i.e. coal \$45 billion per quad and nuclear \$67.5 billion. These figures do not gibe with Ontario Hydro's.

These authors, incidentally, propose that an overall end-use efficiency improved of 1% every 2½ years could sustain a real annual GNP growth of 3% for 30 years. The overall end-use efficiency at the end of the period would only be 20%.

Several large trade unions in the U.S. have completed independent studies which are directly supportive of the arguments made in this book. The Sheet Metal Workers Union concluded that solar heating and cooling in the U.S. could provide a \$2 billion market annually by 1990, creating 20,000 jobs per year. The International Association of Machinists and Aerospace Workers would lead to thousands of new jobs, thus easing the burden of unemployment in the associated industries. A spokesman of the Woodworkers International Union stated "Unions risk disaster and perform a disservice to their members if they do not explore the relationship between energy and jobs."

The American Institute of Architects in an impact study of conservation for new and old buildings referred to earlier, concluded that between 500,000 and 1 million new jobs would result from a conservation programme through 1990. The Federal Energy Administration (FEA-US) has reported that a total U.S. commitment to returnable containers would lead to 117,000 new jobs.

(8) Since space and water heating and cooling represents over 40% of the total energy consumption in Canada the application of solar technology to this demand sector is critical in saving fuels. The Energy Research and Development Administration (ERDA-US) has concluded that present solar technologies for these applications are economically competitive now for regions as far north as Vermont. There seems little question that some 50% of the total demand for space/water heating could be supplied in this way in Canada. This represents a huge total reduction in fuel consumption in Canada.

(9) Conservation and certain renewables have far less land demands and therefore do not compete as much with the other land uses such as farming and recreation.

It is of great significance that the PQ Minister of Energy is in general an advocate of these policies. It remains to be seen where the real political power resides in Quebec.

There seems no way out of the question of public versus private resource exploitation rights. All resources must reside in the public sector, although private development could certainly co-exist, providing it subscribes to stewardship and sustainability principles. This injunction should not be construed as a subscription to traditional socialist theory which may not be relevant to the novelty of current issues. On the other hand, the commitment to equity, domestically and internationally, implies radical restructuring of the concepts of freedom of enterprise, profit and exploitation. One cannot shirk from the recognition that this enlarged public sector implies a radical restructuring of social institutions. This change is not conventional revolution, but perhaps best expressed by Calhoun's spelling "$r_x$evolution" dedicated to non-violence, non-imposed and non-elitist solutions. This vision will probably be acceptable to neither the traditional right nor left.

In summary, the overall strategy to achieve the sustainable society is to proceed in manageable (achievable) steps. Essentially there are two major aspects to these steps. One has to do with policy and one with process. They are not unrelated. The essential policy goal is to maximize conservation. The basic process goal is to achieve participatory processes in the evolution of this policy.

Energy Income Sources
DESPITE THE CONSTANT downplay by energy pushers, solar technology for space and water heating is commercially viable in Canada now. There are institutional and market obstacles to this technology, but these could easily be overcome if the will existed. Despite these obstacles solar business is booming in the U.S. The Energy Research and Development Administration, (ERDA), now the Department of Energy (DOE) has announced that solar residential space and water heating for 12 cities including Boston, New York, Madison and Washington, D.C. is now feasible. That such applications would be suitable in the major cities of Ontario and Quebec is irrefutable.

The urgency of energy policy is determined by the lead times required for supply convesrions. If we are to be serious about a major restructuring of our energy system to be effective, say in 2025, it is urgent to commit ourselves now. This is equally true for conservation as well which is a necessary partner for a future based on renewables. The fact that a solar civilization is technically feasible does not mean it is politically viable. Denis Hayes, in Worldwatch Paper #19, has estimated that to meet 80% of the anticipated world energy budget by 2025 with solar technologies we would require land use of 70 billion square meters for solar collectors, 7.5 million MW(e) of solar cells, 4 times present hydroelectric generation, 5 million wind turbines and a commitment of 15% of the world's forests to creating "energy crops".

Detailed studies have led to conservation/renewables scenarios for Canada, Sweden, the U.S. and California as a state (equivalent to 6th largest industrial country in the world). China, with an extremely aggressive program, now has 5.4 million biogas generators and 60,000 mini-hydroelectric facilities. Brazil is pursuing a policy to have biomass alcohol fuels to equal 100% of imported petroleum by 2000, i.e. 60 billion liters. Australia's goal is 64,000 tons of alcohol per day from wood. Current U.S. Department of Energy goals are to reach prices of electrical power from photovoltaics of $2000 per peak KW by 1980, $500 by 1985 and $100 to $300 by 1990. Current prices are about $6000 per peak KW. Thus electricity from solar cells would be competitive with nuclear by 1980. This will only be fulfilled if there is a major commitment to spur commercial production.

In general, a Canadian initiative in the development of renewable energy technologies would combine the benefits of national and international needs. Foreign aid in the form of the transfer of these appropriate technologies would lend permanent value to our international image. Solar, wind and biomass power would all have great relevance to the countries of Africa, Latin America and the Pacific Rim.

Biomass Conversion
THERE IS LITTLE question that urban sewage and refuse constitutes a valuable source of energy. The possibility of harvesting particular crops such as ocean and land-cultivating kelp for methane production is very interesting. Since 1970, according to Environmentalists for Full Employment, China has constructed 500,000 gas digestors. Scientific research and development in this area could yield a large part of the methane demand in this country. The development of efficient biogas converters particularly with the co-development of high yield bio-fuels and adapted to a number of small stationery and mobile motors could yield a boom export business. Biogas cars, scooters, pumps, mills etc. of varying sizes would have immense and appropriate application in the Third World. Biomass is an indirect form of solar power whereby sunlight is stored in plants which are then harvested and used directly as an energy source or converted to liquid fuels (Liqfuels). The advantages of this system are that we are taking a renewable but diffuse energy income source and converting it to one which can be harvested for sustained and continuous yields. Already certain field crops are economic sources of feedstocks such as methanol, ethanol and ammonia according to Edward S. Lipinsky of Batelle's Columbus Laboratories.

Still another form of biomass is conversion of any organic material, primary or waste, by anerobic digestion, to methane, the major component of natural gas. There are tremendous opportunities in this field from very large operations such as those at feedlots and secondary sewage plants to scaled-down biogas generators for stationery or mobile power.

In Canada the most promising biomass source would be forest products for the production of fuel alcohols to be used in internal combustion engines. Jim Marshall and his colleagues at Environment Canada have calculated that "liqfuels" equivalent to 2.6 quads (twice our total transportation sector demand) are potentially available in Canada. Costs are close to being competitive with gasoline and at a price of $15/bbl of oil we certainly could entertain this as a national project. We now require a full-scale demonstration unit to prove this. However, we could already produce feedstocks economically.

Still other applications of biomass conversion are pyrolysis (decomposition by heat in the absence of oxygen) of organic material, primary or wastes, and direct incineration of garbage or primary organic materials, i.e. wood etc. The obstacles to pyrolysis and incineration are mainly institutional. The industrial-energy complex is simply not interested in diverting their activities from conventional sources and our policies are captives of these multinational giants at present. Yet the potential for biomass conversion in Canada is significant.

As an example of biomass potential it has been reported that only 3% of the area of Ontario devoted to forest production utilizing the bst available growth technology could yield on a *sustainable* basis Ontario Hydro's total planned expansion to 1995. A wood-fuel program maximizing photosynthetic efficiency supported by advanced plant genetics could yield biomass fuel of up to 16 tons per planted acre (and adapted to the Canadian climate). The total tree may be used in this process of modern gasification technology and can provide a clean multi-purpose fuel. Using gas turbine (e.g. Westinghouse PACE 370) one can obtain efficiencies up to 44% through gasification. Moreover, if the forest resource is properly managed, each acre of land can produce fuel indefinitely and at the same time fulfill a multi-purpose role. A gasification programme would require a massive plantation development (about 360 square miles of forest per 1000 MW is required) but economics appear advantageous to this system and the technology is feasible.

Geothermal Power

DEEP PENETRATION into the earth's crust to tap huge reservoirs of geothermal energy could be practical in a decade. Testing by Los Alamos Scientific Laboratory indicates geothermal power will have feasibility and competitiveness with oil by 1990. Instead of drilling deep holes to bury nuclear waste, which uses energy for zero return, we should develop this energy to create geothermal power as a substitute for nuclear for the longer-term.

Wind Power

WIND, LIKE SUN, is a renewable but diffuse source of energy. Nevertheless many parts of the world, including Canada, have the gift of wind resources. Both large and small wind generators have appropriate applications. One of the world's largest units has now been installed in the Magdalen Islands in the Gulf of St. Lawrence. It has a 225 kw capacity and will save 1000 bbls of diesel fuel per year. By the year 2000 it will be feasible to generate 8 billion kwH per year in Canada from wind turbines and mills. This is equivalent to about 1000 MW(e). The cost as indicated by the Science Council of Canada would be very competitive with any other electrical source.

It is very important indeed that we do not develop a double standard whereby we focus on the costs — social, environmental and economic — of "hard" energy paths, but allow them to mysteriously disappear when dealing with the "soft" path. The supporters of pluralistic localism have rested their case on a kind of technological determinism, i.e., the assumption that soft technology is intrinsically a "tool of conviviality" (Illych). This approach carries with it appropriate cultural patterns and values and does not require a technical elite to operate it. The supporters of soft paths often view the electrification trend as a kind of "electro-fascism". None of these arguments are without merit and this author agrees with most of the conclusions but feels that they are little more than unproven assumptions requiring much more analysis and some specialization.

We must be prepared to compare "soft" and "hard" energy paths in terms of total life-cycle costs and replacement costs including comparative social and environmental costs. We must be prepared to defend coal as a "bridging" fossil fuel, a seeming contradiction for proponents of soft paths. But more than anything we must keep our minds and options open, particularly when it is the inflexible and fixed mind sets of the conventionally wise that we are attacking. This is beyond the scope of a single book although books can help. It is to the politics of experience and the experience of politics where we must seek change.

Conclusions

BIGNESS AS AN intrinsic goal has led to grotesque diseconomies of scale. It has led to unprecedented rate and magnitude problems intensified by our exponential myopia. The 1976 Olympics, the James Bay project, the Concorde and nuclear power plants in general, are all illustrative of a unique rate of inflation from first estimate to fianl cost. Not only is prestige confused with power, thus justifying huge cost overruns, but elite decision accompanied by elite accomodation in an environment of non-accountability tends to erode basic principles of a democratic society.

Decentralizing power generation (electrical) generates decentralized political power, so necessary in increasing the rate of turnover of the inventory of attitudes, without which the smooth transition to an ecologically sane society cannot be achieved. Decentralization tends to redistribute policy and decision-making in a more equitable manner. It is a vehicle for the radical extension of participation. It also tends to increase diversity, self-reliance and social and technical innovation, all necessary components for long-term survival. Thus while conservation begins within an existing scheme of "business as usual", based on conventional wisdom, it is instrumental in the necessary transformation of attitudes and institutions towards a society in which social, economic, industrial and ecological systems are closely matched.

A Non-Nuclear Future for Canada

WE ARE ONLY beginning to realize the full costs of nuclear power in Canada. It is now quite clear that every foreign sale has been a loss leader. The scandals over pay-offs for the sales to Argentina and South Korea may be dwarfed by the losses suffered by AECL, the unnatural escalation in costs of Lepreau, La Prade and Gentilly II. We are also witnessing the inevitable unmasking of myths about CANDU. Pickering A is clearly not designed for reasonable safety against a Loss of Coolant Accident (LOCA). Bruce A also has serious problems reflected in the fanatic secrecy regarding the so-called Bruce Safety Notes. The situation is now worse in that AECL, AECB and Ontario Hydro have failed to disclose safety deficiencies to the Porter Commission on Electrical Power in Ontario. The forced resignation of Dr. Foster of AECL is not an answer, just another question. Yet the Canadian government officially continues to support CANDU and throw good money after bad.

What are the "official" plans of the Canadian nuclear establishment? We can get a clear statement from two papers delivered to the SCITEC Parliamentary and Scientific Committee Forum, Ottawa, 1976 by Drs. Mooradian and Aikin, two vice-presidents of AECL.

Firstly, Dr. A.J. Moradian is projecting 130,000 MW(e) from nuclear for the year 2000 despite or in spite of "An Energy Strategy for Canada", EMR's more cautious but official forecast.

This represents 260 individual Pickering units or 216 x 600 MW(e) CANDU's! Not satisfied with this grotesque growth (requiring capital formation of some 300 billion before the year 2000), Dr. Moradian is projecting 900,000 MW(e) for the year 2030 or 1500 x 600 MW(e) CANDU's. Fueling alone for this target will require the equivalent of 150,000 metric tons or uranium per year with *present toal proven* reserves of only some 200,000.

But this is still the good news. The bad news is that Moradian makes it unequivocally clear that a plutonium revovery program and a plutonium-thorium cycle to operate *indefinitely* are the plans of AECL. As a matter of casual technological optimism Moradian indicates that this indefinite fission future would only require 1800 metric tons of thorium feed per year after 2050 to sustain 900,000 MW(e) forever. The critical fossil fuel would be uranium-233 derived from natural thorium, but plutonium would be constantly required as an input.

Now AECL Vice-President, Aikin is more modest and tends to conform more closely to EMR's earlier projections, i.e. about 110,000 MW(e) by 2000. There is a discrepancy between Moradian and Aikin of about 20,000 MW(e). Both exceed EMR projections by significant amounts, 50,000 and 70,000 MW(e). One wonders who represents Canadian energy policy.

The arithmetic of the so-called self-sufficient plutonium-thorium cycle is as follows. For each 100,000 MW(e) of self-sufficient capacity we would require 200 metric tons of thorium per year and a total of 1600 metric tons of plutonium proportioned over the life of the cycle. Canadian cumulative spent fuel will contain about 400,000 kilograms of plutonium by the year 2000 (i.e. 105,000 tons of spent fuel). This amount of plutonium is sufficient to manufacture 40,000 Nakasaki bombs or 80,000 "minimum bombs". The total cumulative plutonium produced by the 900,000 MW(e) for 2030 would be so monstrous as to command disaster. The official AECL policy of a "plutonium economy" is the single most dangerous threat this country faces in the future, politically united or divided. Moreover the uranium-233 economy is qualitatively as hazardous as the plutonium one. U-233 is almost as toxic and Pu-239 and is a weapons grade material when suitably refined.

It is abundantly clear that if we build between 60,000 and 100,000 MW(e) of nuclear generating capacity by the year 2000 we will have totally locked ourselves into a self-fulfilling future of the plutonium economy. The geopolitics of uranium makes this necessary namely we will find ourselves facing uranium supply shortages. We must fuel these plants and the others to follow with plutonium and thorium. We will have backed into a fission forever future.

The fact is that there are risks and uncertainties in all paths to the future. In the end, energy choices are choices between these risks and uncertainties. However, the nuclear risk will not be a deterrent when we hook ourselves into total dependency. The luxury of choice exists now and is short-lived. We can still choose a relatively "soft path" to the future with all its uncertainties, but we must face up to the tragedy of all choice — our world may end with a bang or a whimper.

Nuclear Myths

OUR REJECTION OF nuclear power rests on social, economic and environmental objections. Thes objections can be summarized by examining a set of myths, promulgated by nuclear proponents.

The Canadian nuclear establishment has become isolated in an island of non-credibility. It has not only lost credibility but has become incredible. In many areas the pronouncements and public postures of nuclear proponents in Canada have been thoroughly discredited by formal studies. The myths, so often stated publicly by members of our nuclear establishment, are:

1. *Nuclear power is the only option we have in Canada for the short, medium and long-term.* Eliminating for the present the question of long-term options there are now numerous studies which totally support the view that a nuclear moratorium now would have no adverse effects on social, economic and environmental goals for at least 30 years. Slowing down the rate of energy consumption can be traded off against nuclear power with minimal to zero effects to our "business as usual" future. The above myth is particularly exhorted in "The Nuclear Challenge: Understanding the Debate", The Book Press Limited, Toronto, by Alan Wyatt of the Canadian Nuclear Asociation, but can be found in almost every AECL publication; see also "Nuclear Power in Canada, Questions and Answers", Canadian Nuclear Association, Toronto, 1975.

2. *There are viable means for very long-term storage of high level wastes.* The consensus of all official studies outside Canada is that there are no large-scale economic and technical solutions to this problem. This statement is categorically supported by the Flowers Commission (U.K.), the Burns Report (N.Z.), and the Fox Report (Australia). New studies by the General Accounting Office (U.S.), the U.S. Geological Survey and the California Energy Resources, Conservation and Development Commission affirm the present state of uncertainty but go further by suggesting that there will be no satisfactory solution found. Yet numerous AECL publications or those of the Canadian Nuclear

Association repeat this myth (see "Critical Choice, Nuclear Power in Canada" by Charles Law and Ron Glenn, Corpus, Toronto, 1978, for AECL sources attesting to this myth). But the most shameful expression is the Hare Report sponsored by EMR.

Plutonium would not be the target of terrorists or criminal groups. Numerous studies including those in Australia (Fox Report), U.K. (Flowers Report), New Zealand (Burns Report) and current U.S. policy totally refute this contention. The Mitre Report (U.S.) also deflates this myth and strongly opposes a plutonium economy. President Carter's new policy is an additional significant denial. Incidentally, none of these reports are anti-nuclear, they are merely candid and honest. For this and the following myth see for example "The Nuclear Challenge, Understanding the Debate", by Alan Wyatt of the Canadian Nuclear Association, Book Press, Toronto, 1978.

4. *That plutonium is not the route countries or groups would use to develop nuclear weapons (rather it is enriched uranium).* Again, this simply lacks credibility. A substantive study ERDA 52 (U.S.) and another on behalf of the Union of Civil Liberties (U.K.), the Fox Report (Australia), the Flowers Report (U.K.) and the Mitre Report (U.S.) all disagree with AECL (see Alan Wyatt's book as above). Also see "Nuclear Energy: The Unforgiving Technology" by F.H. Knelman, for further deflation of this myth.

5. *That reactor-grade plutonium is not suitable for the manufacture of nuclear weapons.* The chief weapon designers in the U.S., Carson Mark and Ted Taylor, have totally laid this myth t rest. Also Victor Gillinsky of the U.S. Nuclear Regulatory Commission identifies this as a myth of the nuclear establishment. Yet recently the new president of AECL, Ross Campbell, repeated this myth before the Standing Committee on Natural Resources and Public Works, despite incontrovertible evidence to the contrary.

6. *That plutonium is not so toxic as to be a serious matter of public concern.* Current estimates by official members of nuclear establishments make plutonium one of the most toxic elements in the world when inhaled as a fine particle, possibly second only to Plutonium-210.

Concerning plutonium toxicity there is conflicting evidence about dose-response characteristics. However, even nuclear apologists admit it is extremely lethal when inhaled as small particles and can cause lung cancers.

In order to mediate between extreme views of plutonium toxicity, Dr. Martin Brown of Stanford (a member of NAS's BEIR study) estimates 1 lung cancer per 1 microgram of inhaled, retained plutonium, that is, 1 million lung cancers per gram. He also assumes that $1/10^6$ will likely be released in fuel reprocessing processes and $1/10^5$ will likely reach target cells in the lungs of human populations. Translating this to Canadian inventory by 2000 (400,000 kilograms) we can expect 4000 additional lung cancers to result. Current lung cancer incidence in Canada is about 6000 annually among males.

To quote the most recent study by Bair and Thompson (1975 IAEA) a dose of more than $16.3 \times 10\text{-x}$ gms would eventually cause premature death from a lung cancer in beagles and "it seems clear cancer might occur at lower levels..."; "$268 \times 10\text{-x}$ gms could ultimately cause 1 lung cancer /8 persons (if humans are as susceptible as rats)."

Translating this latter statement to the Canadian production of plutonium in the year 2000 (400,000 kgs) we could have an additional burden of 17,600 cases of lung cancer per year. This represents a huge increase over the present rate (6000 per 20 million for males).

That solar and other renewables are not viable for Canada and can contribute very little to our national energy demand in the next 25 years. "Energy Policy and the Conservation Option", the earlier section in this chapter, totally refutes this position so often repeated by utilities and nuclear agencies. ERDA (U.S.) has completed studies indicating viability of solar energy for cities such as Boston and Milwaukee. Surely these studies make solar space/water heating applicable to most Canadian cities. Even our own EMR is now engaged in a substantial program of some $380 million to promote renewables.

That nuclear power is cheaper than other competing sources (and increases in capital costs equal the inflation rate). The facts indicate that nuclear power plants are inflating at about 20% per year. Pickering #1 ($175m) would now cost up to $800m to build, but inflation would only make up 25% of this. Gentilly II has a similar inflation rate. Original and present costs of Lepreau and Gentilly II indicate their inflation is *twice* that of monetary inflation. This is also true of La Prade, the heavy water plant in Quebec, now abandoned. A recent report in the U.S. (the Ryan Report) found that nuclear power plants are "prohibitively expensive and hazardous."

9. *That the* CANDU *reactor is intrinsically safer than its competitors.* The secret document prepared by the Argonne National Laboratories on CANDU clearly indicates that (a) there are many unanswered safety problems; (b) CANDU is more likely to have a core-meltdown that LWR's (but less likely to have a "worst case accident", i.e. escape of radioactive inventory). CANDU is particularly vulnerable to seismic events. The *secret* study by Ontario Hydro for AECB (1976) indicates Pickering A safety deficiencies against a Loss of Coolant Accident (LOCA).

The *secret* Bruce Safety Notes throw doubts on Bruce A's safety. Moreover there has been a cover-up of these safety defects by AECL, AECB and Ontario Hydro, revealed by Dr. Gordon Edwards of the Canadian Coalition for Nuclear Responsibility and decried by Dr. Porter, chairman of Ontario's Royal Commission on Electrical Power.

10. *That nuclear power is appropriate for export to developing countries.* ERDA #52 (U.S.) is the most substantive document to refute this proposal. Even that global nuclear pusher, the International Atomic Energy Agency, (IAEA) admits nuclear power will contribute insignificantly to global energy equity by the year 2000. The fact is that well over 90% of all nuclear trade, including reactors and fuels will continue to be between economically developed countries.

11. *That nuclear power plant decommissioning is neither necessary nor expensive.* Since Canada has had no experience in decommissioning plants, this view is totally inadmissible. The U.S. has ample experience and reckons the cost at $100m per commercial plant, using entombment, a preferred method. By using mothballing and dismantling, capital costs are lower but maintenance costs go on for hundreds of years. (For this myth see "Critical Choice, Nuclear Power in Canada" by Charles Law and Ron Glenn, Corpus, Toronto, 1978).

12. *That we can build 130,000 MW(e) of installed nuclear generating plants by the year 2000.* This is not possible in terms of the necessary rate of capital formation and the demand for material and human resources. This alarming projection is being made with total irresponsibility by AECL and should be publicly disavowed. If one adds individual projections of all provincial utilities these add up to some 100,000 MW(e) by 2000. This could cost a total of $200 billion by 2000. It represents a 1600% increase over installed capacity in 1978.

13. *That electrical energy demand must be projected at 7% per year far into the future.* The U.S. and Europe's experience makes this a tragic and foolhardy proposition. By restricting electricity to appropriate end-use and by managing demand, consumption may easily be reduced to 3% per year or less by 1995. For a clear example of electro-fetishism or even electro-fascism see Alan Wyatt's book, myth #3.

14. *That "proven" uranium reserves in Canada are 400,000 metric tons.* The above figure is a "potential" not a "proven" reserve, and yet members of the nuclear establishment constantly confuse the two. The problem is that as uranium ores decrease in metal content a point is reached where net energy rather than cost is the limiting factor; that is it takes too much energy to recover the uranium.

15. That the CANDU *reactor does not produce more plutonium than almost all of its leading competitors.* ERDA #52 (U.S.), the Argonne National Laboratories Report on CANDU and the Swedish International Peace Research Institute both attest to the fact that CANDU produces about 50% more plutonium per generating capacity than its leading competitors (except Magnox, a British reactor).

16. That reprocessing (removing plutonium) solves the problem of high level waste and controlling radium solves the problem of mining waste. These are both categorically untrue since plutonium continues to be formed from certain trans-uranic actinudes and radium from thorium. Moreover there are serious plutonium releases from reprocessing plants as experienced in the U.S.

Given these 16 myths and their refutation, nuclear power is more costly and more socially and environmentally objectionable in the long run than any other current source of energy. Reliance on the atom is undesirable compared to conservation and renewables in the medium future. Nuclear power is already more costly than coal in certain regions. An excellent source book documenting many of these myths is "Critical Choice, Nuclear Power in Canada" by Charles Law and Ron Glenn, Corpus, Toronto, 1978; also see AECL publications of speeches by W.B. Lewis, J.S. Foster and J.L. Gray.

The Arithmetic of the Conservation/Solar Option

ASSUMING A LARGE conservation program, we could easily increase the gross national energy efficiency, first law efficiency, from 50% to 75% (technical "fix" scenario). Or to put this another way, we could save 25% of our projected supply by the year 2000. And still another way of viewing this is that it represents a total energy growth of about 1.5% per year over the next 22 years. This level of conservation can be achieved without modifying or impeding our projected social, economic and environmental goals. In addition, we would supply half of our national space and water heating from renewable sources, i.e. about 20% of our total national consumption. If we assume a consumption figure of 8 Quad (10^{15} Btu) in the year 2000, this would translate into 1.6 Quad from solar, 2 Quad from hydro, 0.4 Quad from other renewable sources and 1 Quad from on-site generation. This would leave 3 Quad from all other sources. In addition, there would be a conservation saving of 4 Quad in the year 2000. This saving would leave 3 Quad to be supplied by other sources. Translating this need into gas, oil or coal amounts to 3 trillion cubic feet (tcf) of gas, 1.4 million barrels a day (mbd) of oil or 140 million tons per year of coal. If these resources contributed in the ratio 1 to 2 to 3 we would then require 0.5 tcf gas, 0.47 mbd oil and 47 million tons of coal. Given proven plus potential reserves of these three fossil fuels of 610 tcf gas, 90 billion barrels of oil (excluding heavy oils and synthetic crude) and 120 billion tons of coal, static reserves of all three are of the order of 1000 years.

Examining our position in the year 2000, and assuming that in the 22 years from 1978 we consumed at the above rates, the accumulated consumption of gas, oil and coal would be 11 tcf, 10mbd and 1 billion tons. This is the really good news, for these quantities are small fractions of proven reserves. Even if we extend our use of fossil fuels to the year 2035 at reduced rates of about 1.5% per year, on the average we will still not have consumed our proven reserves.

Canada can thus be assumed to be self-sufficient in energy resources, provided we restrict total energy growth for the next 57 years to 1.5% per year. Not only can we manage at this growth projection, but we can do so with no increase in present nuclear capacity and no interference with social, economic and environmental goals. Actually, we are convinced we can reduce energy consumption to zero by 2035.

In 1975 Canada consumed about 0.33×10^9 Btu per capita. Assuming that 75% of this per capita consumption can provide all the goods and services necessary to serve the needs of 40 million people, then total energy consumption in 2035 would be about 10 Quad. Our goal should be close to a sustainable society by that time; i.e. zero growth in population and energy consumption. Our total fossil fuel reserves by 2035 will still amount to over 500 tcf gas, 80 bbls oil and 111 billion tons of coal, a total of 2800 Quad or 280 years of total fossil fuel reserves. However we are proposing that over 50% be from renewables.

There is no question that what we have proposed here does not have the merits of a fully developed scenario. Moreover, even such fully developed scenarios incorporating economic modelling would be prone to intrinsic inadequacies of all "ill-structured problems". The work of David Brooks ("Some Scenarios of Energy Demand in Canada in the Year 2025", EMR, April 20, 1977) and Amory Lovins ("Exploring Energy-Efficient Futures for Canada", Conserver Society Notes, May-June 1976, Science Council of Canada) also are pregnant with these intrinsic uncertainties. Finally, there is the important aspect of whether in fact we can or should dvelop a sustainable society in Canada isolated from the rest of the world. In particular, we cannot avoid the powerful ties we have with the U.S. Nor should we deny our obligation to share in the development of global equity. Nevertheless, in broad principle, the attempt to move in the direction of indpendent sustainability has both direct and indirect spin-off values for everybody. A significant long-term reduction in consumption per capita, a levelling-off of all growth, the development of a renewables society and the experiments in social ecology could all enhance our capacity for meaningful and appropriate aid trade and technology transfer.

Explicit end-point economic and demographic assumptions are a stable population of 40 million in 2035 and an average real economic growth rate of 1% per year over the entire 57 years from 1978. In terms of the phased stages, stage #1 would aim at average economic growth rates of 3%, stage #2 of 2% and stage #3 of 1%. Population in the year 2000 would be about 30 million and in 2035 about 40 million or growth rates between 1978 and 2000 would be about 1% average and between 2000 and 2035 would taper to zero. Average total energy growth in the three stages is estimated at 1.5%, 1% and achieving zero by 2035. Electrical growth would decline from 2.8% to a constant supply ratio of less than 18%. Some of this would be available from solar and other renewables.

Some Barriers to the Conservation Option
A CENTRAL, IF NOT dominant, aspect of the energy crisis in Canada and the U.S. is the apparent incapacity to optimize investment in energy supply and conservation. A further complication is the differential growth in electrical supply and total energy, leading to an inexorable development of an electrical economy. Moreover, despite this traditionally higher growth in electrical supply, two major contradictions persist:

(1) transportation remains dominantly fuel-based, as do many chemicals, plastics etc., with no radical movement to substitution;

(2) elecricity as a high-grade energy source is being mismatched with end-use in new housing stock by being applied to space and water heating, a wasteful application.

The net result of the above is not a decreased dependency on oil and gas through this high growth of electrical supply but rather a greater dependency, and, therefore vulnerability, as imports increase. In a more subtle way the huge commitment to electrical growth pushes the entire energy supply system forward at a rate incompatible with the capacity of capital formation, capital itself being a scarce resource. One cannot argue that economic viability is negatively correlated to this wasteful growth in energy supply with its powerful distorting effects on the entire social and environmental systems. The net effect is that the costs of growth exceed the benefits.

The crux of a rational energy policy should be a radical reduction in electrical supply growth, restricting electricity more and more to appropriate (obligatory) end-uses. There must also be a shift from costly central generation to on-site generation. Such policies accompanied by the utilization of the many means available for fuel conservation could achieve the same net output of goods and services as we enjoy today at much lower capital and environmental costs. We never get a free lunch, but the one proposed is more nutritious and equally ample, at less cost.

The barriers to the conservation option are profound and entrenched in the nature of the market economy itself. For one thing, investment capital for conservation from that for general manufacturing operates under different rules. While the ultimate return on capital and on energy is clearly superior for conservation, the accepted debt-to-equity ration is distinctly lower than that for the maintenance and expansion of productive capacity. The comparison with utilities exacerbates the situation. Utilities, whether public or private, are directly or indirectly protected by regulating risk, by direct or indirect social subsidy and by a growth orientation, i.e. power yields power. Return on capital (payback) for utilities can be deferred or even deficit budgetted. The result is that the "free market" cannot optimize the allocation of capital between two distinct energy options — conservation and energy supply.

A further factor is that even where payback for conservation is less than 5 years (as it is in many cases) the price system tends to favour the lowest initial cost, ignoring life cycle costs. This tendency is as true for consumers (public) as it is for industry, where discretionary requirements are a deterrent to conservation investment.

Household insulation, commercial insulation, air conditioning, refrigeration (where lifecycle efficiencies vary by a factor of 2 with a cost variation of 30%), waste heat recuperation, cogeneration, on-site generation and heating, etc. are all victimized by the market. And it is not the "free market" but a distorted market that does the victimizing.

Given the built-in distortions of the market (high direct or indirect subsidies for energy supply, plus the existence of cartels) the only answer is a counter-distortion of the market to re-allocate capital resources for energy optimally between supply and conservation. Pricing energy on its actual energy content or taxing energy is not a sufficient lever because the energy contribution to value-added in the manufacturing sector averages 10% or less nationally. Traditional pricing of electricity is based on average rather than incremental costs and this again tends to distort the market. Moreover, higher prices pose an equity problem and tend to punish the poor while the wealthy are not inhibited in their consumption. Rationing on the other hand could be effective with equity clauses. However, this is a clear crisis strategy. Electrical energy is the critical supply sector most affected by the above forces. Moreover electricity is the most capital-intensive even though the most valuable of energy sources. A major problem is the misuse of electricity, i.e., the mismatch of this high-grade source for low-grade end-uses, i.e. space and water heating. The almost universal principle of implacably increasing electrical supply (always at about twice the growth rate of total energy), while retaining a major inventory of plant and product that intrinsically relies on fossil fuels, leads inevitably to the misuse of electricity. There is also increased dependency on these same fuels through the multiplier effect of supply, which must create demand. We become "hooked" by excessive energy-intensive growth which is inflationary and job destroying, i.e. we are "hooked" by a losing game. Our primary task is therefore to change the game.

One solution to this problem might be a reversal of role-playing by mandate. The utilities would be mandated to play the major role in conservation, through regulated rate structures, through the application of conservation hardware and through a necessary matching of source and end-use. The utilities could actually profit from such conservation. A further incentive could be to enter the cogeneration market. Now there are built-in restrictions against cogeneration. Applying on-site cogeneration of electricity and steam in just three industries in Canada — paper, chemicals and petroleum products and refining could generate 30% of all our electricity. This shift from central generation to on-site generation coupled to district heating is desirable. Utilities should be mandated to purchase excess cogenerated electricity. West Germany obtains 18% of its electrical needs from cogeneration, compared to perhaps 1 or 2% in Canada. By a combination of changing roles and rules, i.e. distorting the market so it encourages investment in conservation, we might solve a basic problem of energy. Society must pay a premium for deferring gratification ths extending the validity of life cycle efficiencies and life cycle costs. This should be carrots to those industries which conserve and sticks for those who do not.

Since about 40% of our industrial energy consumption, or about 12% of our total secondary energy, is used in the form of process steam, the potential savings from cogeneration are very great. Assuming 50% conversion to cogeneration we can save 6% of our total energy. A scenario of a massive conservation program (MCP) combining high pay-off conservation measures, such as cogeneration, waste-heat recuperators, district heating combined cycles, trash incinerator heat recovery, methane from organic wastes, etc., could easily reduce our projected electrical power growth by 50% up to 1990. Total secondary energy consumption could be reduced to out 1975 level with help of such measures and we could still maintain an acceptable real GNP growth of 3%. Many reliable reports indicate that the capital savings as between energy supply and conservation is about $25b per annual Quad in favour of the latter and even higher in the comparison between nuclear generation and the use of waste heat or waste combustibles (over $35b per annual Quad). If, for example, we supply 5 Quad by nuclear power rather than by waste heat utilisation it would cost $175b more per year! If we had introduced a massive conservation program (MCP) in 1972, by 1990 we would have had capital savings of over $80b as compared to projected demand, i.e. an average of $1.6b per year saved. Since both capital and energy are scarce resources this conservation option is the best energy policy.

Reducing total new electrical construction to 1990 by 50%, i.e. to about 20,000 MW(e) then on-site forms could make up 50% of ths new plant, leaving only 10,000 MW(e) additional to be supplied by other sources. Hydro capacity under construction in Canada exceeds this additional 10,000 MW(e) and thus it is quite clear that we require no more nuclear power. Scenarios in the U.S. have supported the contention that projected new electrical power plant construction to 1990 could be halved and 50% of this half could be provided by on-site sources. The MCP scenario's most impressive dividend is a reduction in oil and gas demand which could extend the lifetime of our reserves. Preliminary estimates indicate that by 1990 we could reduce natural gas demand by 0.5 Quads per year and oil demand by almost 1 Quad per year (over 165 million barrels of oil). Total fuel savings of 1.5 Quads represent a significant proportion of our primary fuel consumption.

Central generation rests on the myth of unlimited economies of scale. Economies of scale are real up to the point where a marginal increase scale leads to a level of diminished return that is uneconomical. This is as true of insulation as of power plants.

There is a powerful group in this country who believe in the myth of the free market and who preach a "hands off" or laissez faire program that allows us to make profits through the mystique of the invisible hand. While they constantly distort the market these powerbrokers uphold its freedom as sacred. It is not an accident that this same group usually adopts the timeworn tenets of rugged individualism so insensitive to group or race inequities. "Business as usual" has always meant "muddling through". When growth happened to be robust the muddling became principle and the periods of recession were omitted from the analysis. The "invisible hand" has become the invisible finger of fate performing an unmentionable act on society.

The market system is not designed to deal with the value of durability, lifetime cost and efficiency, the relative content of labour and energy insensitivity and the delayed, deferred or indirectly subsidized social costs. On the contrary, only the perceived initial cost, devoid of lifetime and intergenerational costs, is an essential market dynamic. To a degree the market controls services as well, so that only non-deferred, i.e. immediate gratificaton is involved in transactions. Energy shortages and rising costs have somewhat altered this pattern because high energy-using consumer goods are now viewed in terms of operating costs as well as initial capital costs thus reflecting efficiency to a degree; the automobile is an example. But such pricing is still far short of incorporating total lifetime costs and is still geared to relatively short time horizons.

The market inhibits the broader application of the conservation/renewables option for the above reasons. Coupled to this the energy establishment both through conventional wisdom and direct interests are neglecting the opportunities of the conservation/renewables alternative. Insulation may be an exception. This is regrettable but understandable. It therefore seems inescapable that the public sector must bear the major responsibility for encouraging and implementing conservation applications and renewables development. Otherwise both the producer and consumer will remain locked into the present traditional energy developments and the market system which reinforces them.

A combination of incentives and disincentives, of tax credits and penalties, together with low-interest, long-term loans (possibly integrated with restructural utility rates to penalize excess consumption and reward conservation) can catalyze the transition to the conservation/renewables option.

The transfer from central generation to various forms of on-site generation, coupled to end-use matching is the major conservation option and the critical strategy for improved national energy efficiency. On-site generation implies the virtual discontinuation of electrical resistive space heating. Our goal by the year 2000 should be to reduce the electricity fraction of our total energy demand to 25%, with further reductions down to totally obligatory uses in 2035. The Thermo Electron Corporation (see Technology Review, June 1977, pp. 31-40) has established the reasonable feasibility of reducing total new generating capacity by 60% with current technology and providing most of this capacity from on-site generating stations.

Relative costs of on-site generation range from 40 to 30% of total system costs for central plants. Translating this to the Canadian situation we could reduce projected new generating plants from about 120,000 MW(e) to about 40,000 MW(e) with 30,000 MW(e) from on-site sources by the year 2000. The investment saving would be about 87 billion dollars.

Between now and 1990 we could easily save 2 Quads per year, largely from new automobile fuel economy standards, on-site generation, improved industrial efficiency, improved appliance efficiency standards and improved insulation. These changes represent an accumulated saving of 24 Quad in 12 years.

A striking advantage of our scheme is the drastic reduction in the necessary capital formation. By shifting capital drastically from supply to conservation (and from central to on-site generation) we should be able to reduce the required capital by more than 50% to the year 2000 without any serious change in our real standard of living (actually with a better mix of quality and quantity). Another striking advantage will be dramatic reductions in the demand for fossil fuels.

By improving national average energy end-use efficiencies to about 20% by the year 2000 we could sustain a real economic growth of 37% at least through 1990. GNP per unit of primary energy could be increased by 50% in the same time frame and then continue to gain as energy efficiency increased more rapidly than GNP. The composition of the GNP would also undergo radical changes as services grew more rapidly than goods production.

Total savings for our energy scenarios to the year 2000 would be about 87 billion in electrical generation and about 40 billion from all other conservation measures (over and above standard growth projections of standard forms). 127 billion in 27 years represents about 5½ billion per year. This could provide one million persons with a guaranteed annual income (GAI) of $5500 per year. Savings from drastic military reduction could provide a roughly equal amount. This would provide the base for our GAI scheme (see previous chapter).

We have argued that energy futures are highly determining of social futures. It is for this reason that we have placed so much emphasis on an energy scenario that leads to sustainability. Transitional policy has two major components — conservation and renewables development.

Conclusions

THE KEY LONG-TERM policy goal is to achieve zero net energy growth by the year 2035. If this goal is not achieved and we are still a growth society, we will run out of flexible options particularly the "soft path" to the future. We are then locked into a growth society with either a long-term plutonium-239 and uranium-233 economy or fusion. The choice will be breeders or fusion, both high technologies. The lines of implacable choice are already drawn. Depending on how quickly we can react and decide — and there is very little leaway left — we can still choose between two radically different futures. Twenty-five years is the approximate lifetime of uranium, oil and natural gas used together at high growth rates. If we maximize the pursuit of this route, maximizing both fissile and fossil fuel utilization we will reach the year 2000 locked into an inventory of hardware, software and attitudes totally dependent on breeding or fusing, i.e. on nuclear futures possibly with coal as the last of the fossil fuels.

The conservation-solar option involves virtually zero risk to the year 2000. At the worst we are taking a calculated risk of some minimal lost time should non-nuclear replacement technologies not emerge in the next 22 years. We can maintain existing stockpiles of uranium and non-functioning nuclear plants which could then be started up immediately if that were the future decision. On the other side the risk is incalculable and unacceptable. The legitimizing of a plutonium-uranium-233 economy represents a point of no return.

Not only are we recommending a policy trade-off between nuclear and conservation/renewables but we are also proposing that the capital being formed for the various nuclear programs including R & D in Canada be diverted to these alternatives. This proposal seems entirely feasible since we are dealing with public funds in all cases whether federal or provincial. Since there is impeccable evidence that the necessary rate of capital formation for the conservation/renewable option is significantly less than for nuclear, this proposal should include significant savings and thus be far less inflationary. We fully realize that there are social costs involved in such radical transfers of policy and we would propose that compensation and opportunity be preferentially granted to the involved groups, both corporate and labour.

What we are proposing is a short nuclear moratorium followed by a phased withdrawal paced to equal the rate of replacement of savings and alternatives. There is no pretense that conversions from one energy source to another, or for that matter, conservation itself, are without social costs. These are largely the normal costs of technological change with its concomitant dislocation and discontinuity of capital and labour. The automobile destroyed the buggy manufacturers and the raising of horses to draw the buggies. But the new auto bodies and combustion horsepower soon replaced them. Society did not accept the responsibility to compensate the losers. We are recommending that such social compensation be accepted in the conversion to the conservation/renewables option. This should include the costs of the transfer and retraining of labour, technical and non-technical, the protection of the unions' jurisdictional status quo and the right of first opportunity to the corporate sectors displaced. A fraction of the capital saved through the alternative option should be directed for compensation. Unless the threat of change is largely reduced the institutional obstacles to it will survive. The change will occur in any case, but at greater cost to everyone.

In closing down nuclear power plants we are saving some of the costs of decommissioning and high level waste management. We can save all those parts of the plant involved in electrical generation. These can be converted to other fuels.

Pickering, Bruce and Gentilly II can be "turned down" in phase with the conservation-solar replacement. In the event that it is clearly perceived by 1990 or 1995 that our conservation/ renewable program is not feasible then they can be "turned on".

Quebec's new white paper on energy policy contains both good and bad news. The good news is conservation orientation. The bad news is overemphasis on electricity and over reliance on Hydro Quebec.

Chapter 7

Anti-Nation:
The Vision of a Sustainable Society

WE ARE CLOSING our book with a vision of the future, a society which completes the transition scenario as we have described it, adopts the appropriate energy policy and attains the status of sustainability. To describe this new society we have coined the term anti-nation. We make no pretension that ours is more than a preliminary and exploratory conceptual model of a new form of state, which is designed both for survival and commitment. It is integrated with the major thrust of this book in that the internal design of anti-nation based on restructuring sub-systems is consistent with national and international survival.

Anti-nation is a survival concept for Canada describing a country with the following characteristics:

(1) Achieving long term stability through principles of sustainability and therefore having high survival value. This stability would involve a radical transformation of technology, culture, economics and politics, based on ecological principles.

(2) Serving as a viable example, model, experiment or pattern for other nation-states in the economically developed world and for the world as a whole. Nevertheless each nation would correctly cherish its own version as all would cherish diversity. The aim is to achieve a blend of independence and interdependence within a broad consensus over the ecological imperative.

(3) Including in its organizational structures, built-in mechanisms to ensure the ultimate withering away of its own national identity and its merging into an inter- and trans-national global community. (The prerequisites for this will be a powerful set of international commitments and initiatives). It

will mean the replacement of economic imperatives by ethical and ecological imperatives. A contradiction is recognized between the conflicting needs to protect individual dignity and the global community.

(4) Disavowing power in all its forms — symbolic, ritualistic and physical as well as political and military. Anti-nation is a state which espouses powerlessness, which divests itself of flags and anthems, armies and "intelligence" services, which disposes of class power, male power, money power and white power.

(5) Encouraging diversity, community and decentralizing policy and decision-making with full participation of all citizens. The last growth area of human development will be never ending.

What do we mean by anti-nation? We do not mean non-nation. We recognize that sovereignty can only be relinquished or shared if one first has it genuinely. By anti-nation we mean a nation-state, i.e. a social, political, economic, territorial and psychological community, organized and directed on lines directly opposite to those which characterize nationalism. In a way anti-nation is analagous to anti-matter in physics. Anti-nation is a state negative to the traditional imperatives and forms of power, policy and persuasion. Anti-nation is a set of policies and priorities which are geared internally to national ecological sanity and externally to global ecological sanity.

Anti-nation is a concept of a state in which all the norms of nationhood are eliminated or inverted. To understand the opposite we must elucidate that to which it is opposed. A nation-state is characterized by the privilege of closed boundaries and the means to enforce authority and sovereignty. It is founded on the notion of power as the exclusive instrument of purpose. It has both symbolic and real tools to exercise this national right, all the way from flag and anthems to intelligence (spy) agencies and armies. It is founded on mistrust. The ultimate crime is subversion. Loyalty is an ultimate need, loyalty beyond all other considerations save passport identity of national origin. It is the extension of my family to my country above all others, right or wrong.

All of this is outside of current and traditional ideology or even the present nature of social systems. Under the existing spectrum of nation-states differing social systems will stress collective or social rights over individual ones while others stress the reverse. The socialist and communist states tend to the former while the capitalist states prescribe to the latter. Rightist dictatorships tend to deny both kinds of rights although they are usually overt supporters of big corporations who are their major allies. But all these types of states have the major and essential

136

characteristics of being consumed by maintaining at all costs their limited sovereignty although they may wish to extend it. Absolute rights pertain to the state within its borders including its right to use or abuse its land or people. To defend these rights these states use armies and secret police, internal and external. These states also exhibit their territorial imperatives by proxy through international sports or prestige projects. The Olympics is a war by other means. The Concorde, CANDU, James Bay are all forms of national ego. It is the negation of all these characteristics of nationhood that we mean by anti-nationhood.

At this point it is important to discuss some of the preconditions of anti-nationhood and illustrate how Canada fulfills them. Canada is distinctive among Western industrial states in its extremely large territory (3 million square miles), its relatively small population (22 million or about 30,000 square miles per capita), its immense wealth in natural resources, and its international political image. Canada is a middle-sized power politically, with a reputation, not always validly earned, for a mediating role among the super-powers. It is also a relatively new nation. Not being an infant nation or a mini-nation and not being middle-aged, old or ancient, Canada can at once avoid the political rabies of vociferous nationalism and chauvinism and the traditional techniques of power. So far, Canada has not lost its cool in international affairs, although its intrinsic bi-national status creates an internal political problem that could be settled amicably if the will existed on both sides, as we have described in an earlier chapter, at the expense of short-term interests, practicality, so-called "real" politics, expediency or all the other terms we use when we desert principles and abdicate the "responsibility to endure." And of course, by anti-nation we mean the new and necessary revolutionary state (Jacques Ellul) that optimizes the survival and fulfillment of the individual and the community.

What will be the more detailed characteristics of an anti-nation? The total restructuring of the four basic subsystems will be involved — politics, economics, technology and culture. We deal with each of these in turn.

The Politics of Non-Politics
IN MANY WAYS the politics of anti-nation are non-politics, mainly in their rejection of traditional parties, constituencies, decision-making and power. This new politics will involve profound changes in internal and external postures and policies. Politics and economics are inseparable. The major aim for anti-nation is to redirect our political-economy to higher social purpose, and break the lock-in malfunction which leads to the exclusive ends

of increased growth and power.

The fact that we are subjectively many nations must be recognized objectively and our constitution so altered as to create a multi-national state, which is a compromise between the absolute separatists on the one hand and the absolute federalists on the other. All member nations in the multi-national state would have the right to secede, but under precise, pre-agreed terms. Each nation would pursue its own diverse forms of cultural expression, while evolving towards a bilingual state. Cultural diversity, like individual diversity, would also be encouraged within each member nation. Nevertheless, each member nation would sacrifice much of its equity, energy and environmental sovereignty to a single federal authority in which equality of representation would be ensured. Solution of the problems of regional disparity and multi-nationalism in Canada would be a major contributor to solving global problems since these are the same issues that divide the world. The federal politics and economics of this multi-national state would be anti-nationhood.

Our political structures would have to be radically altered to involve all our citizens in the democratic process. We might experiment with a single party system in which the government remains in power for a period of up to eight years, but with the proviso that nobody at the Cabinet level, including the Prime Minister, could seek re-election. This would enable a government to govern and not to be pressured to manipulate and manoeuver for re-election. A complex system of safeguards to prevent abuse and corruption of power would have to be developed and an ultimate value placed on the traditional human freedoms. All people running for election would have equal access to public funds and the media, and no access to private donations.

On the question of military power, Canada, as an anti-nation, should be the first political state to totally disavow military power and to avow moral power. This means both offensive and defensive aspects of the military since much of the contemporary military technology blurs the distinction between the two. Nuclear power has rendered war obsolesecent in that nobody can win although unfortunately not obsolete. We have to help make it extinct. The only ultimate pattern for survival is the concept of humankind as a unitary species. Modern military and communications technology unifying the world by virtue of their global reach simply affirms this and survival now depends on cooperation, not competition. The threat also makes it incumbent on us to affirm that we are all each other's brothers, sisters and keepers.

Canada should become the first political entity dedicated in its internal and external policies to total and complete disarmament — not just by word but by deed. We should disband all our armed forces, army, navy and air force. By all means let us be kind to the generals — pay them a pension, at least the old ones who once had a function and fulfilled it. Let them keep their medals of past service but all our awards should be for peace and justice.

On the other hand, Canada should extend its international U.N. peace-keeping role, preferably in ways more innovative than the military — a volunteer unarmed peace corps with multiple functions but dedicated to mediation and non-violence. This proposal re our military is made in the interest of our individual and collective security.

Canada should achieve zero population growth and the development of superior and safer population control techniques. Population control must evolve through people's commitment and will, not by coercion. This means a vast national information and educational program involving every citizen in the country. A good beginning was made in the hearings and conference of the C.C.R.E.M. (Canadian Council of Resource and Environmental Ministers).

Participation by the people in the decision-making process is also the basic prerequisite for environmental control. We should, with respect to the environment, have a long period of pre-assessment of environmental impacts before the introduction of any new and particularly large technology. At the same time, we should establish the principle of public and open hearings where the people can hear the full airing of the arguments on cost-benefit and risk-benefit balances.

While we have not labelled population as one of our most critical problems for reasons stated earlier, we must affirm its reality and relative priority. We believe there is a "population bomb" in Africa, Asia and parts of Latin America that is outgrowing the food supply. Agricultural productivity and processes are counterproductive and the cities of the poor are exploding. The nuclear military arsenal is an example of a grotesque capacity for over-kill and over-skill urbanization coupled with huge disamenities. Foreign aid continues to be counterproductive and we have sold these countries our own losing games. The answer is not population control by technology. The answer is self-help aid and appropriate development, as well as practising what we preach, i.e. limiting our own population growth as policy. Unfortunately, the "lifeboat ethic" won't wash or float. Drowning people will pull everybody down with them. It is as much our problem as theirs, not for altruism but for survival.

The emergence of trans-national, non-governmental organizations (NGO's) has already played a major role and had a major impact on the movement for world peace and social development. The nuclear disarmament movement directly contributed to the atmospheric test ban treaty. The various black groups, women's groups, native peoples' groups etc. have all contributed to the general raising of consciousness and the real amelioration of sexism and racism. The world environmental movement has played a major role in sensitizing the public and moving the politician to respond to the environmental crisis. Public interest scientists, lawyers and doctors have all had positive impacts on upgrading services and products. In general, the various NGO's have acted as the front line of the necessary change in attitudes and values regarding peace, justice, consumer rights, racial equality and environmental concern. The main technique is to use available but often hoarded information to reveal contradictions and anomalies in the system.

Citizens' movements have also revolutionized social structure, organization, function and role by revitalizing non-hierarchal and participatory democracy. The stage has been reached where networking between groups must increase effectiveness and when coalitions of these movements must translate their activities into political processes. At the very least these new movements must invade municipal politics, the area most amenable to intervention. More and more they must become policy-oriented and concerned more with viable alternatives than social criticism. In the longer run, both the form of non-hierarchal or horizontal hierarchy and the technique of consensus, networking and participation will shape the political process of the future.

Diversity and Cohesion — A Culture of Community

THE EVOLUTION INTO a sustainable society, steady-state antination would hopefully overcome the endless dichotomy between individual and society, between personal and social needs and between the jurisdictions and sovereignties of nations and of the planet. This development would have to be accompanied by the evolution of creative leisure so that working and playing were a continuum as well as a change. That is, leisure should be useful and work enjoyable. There would be no unemployment, but the concept of "job" or of "being gainfully employed" would have to change radically from the influence of the "work ethic" to that of the psycho-social ethic. The distinction between self-learning and formal learning would have to be erased. Gordon Rattray Taylor in his remarkable book

"Rethink" talks of the Buddhist's concept of the functions of work as:

(1) To help us develop our faculties.

(2) To overcome self-centredness and allow us to join together as a community engaged in common, cooperative tasks.

(3) To produce the goods and services required by a "becoming" society (becoming rather than "doing" or "being" and therefore not just the conventional GNP).

There is enormous wisdom in this trio of functions representing the cultural development of the Third World, for it encompasses most of the psychic nutrition we require for survival and development. Instead of a homogenous mass society without individual diversity and differentiation we could have a community society with what Ivan Illich calls a "convivial" life-style. A community society is one whose bonds are voluntary. All individuals in such a society are at once themselves and part of all others. In this kind of society there is a diversity coupled to equality and community. The mass-society, on the other hand, is at once undifferentiated and atomized. Each individual is identical yet alone.

One cannot overstress the value of a community society. There is an accumulating body of historical and anthropological evidence that this kind of society does not just incorporate a simple kind of stability, but that the stability exacts a profound effect on the behaviour of all its members. Each individual in the community society has enhanced stability and enhanced capacity. The effect is to strengthen the individual's capacity to cope while at the same time stabilizing the community as a whole. The enhanced stability does not restrict the internal capacity to grow and develop, but acts as a catalyst for such growth.

But to return to the issue of work, a community society might well have some of the characteristics of certain primitive communal societies. This means that everyone has a function. Some people would have an economic function (a production of physical needs or goods and services) and others non-economic — creative, artistic, even self-learning and expressing). The various functions are not differentiated in social value, because they are all viewed as either protecting the present or preserving the future. In terms of incomes there would be no distinction between work and self-attainment. That is, social utility would be equally distributed between those who produce goods or services and those who create, invent and learn. The social system would evolve into a free association of humans into their self-designated concept of family. The children would be the children of the community, with schooling between equals whether they be learners or teachers and totally free of sexism

141

or racism with free choices of religion, occupation, etc. This stage in the evolution of an anti-nation would take more than one generation, of course, but it would be necessary for long-term survival. Diversity in all forms of people and institutions would be encouraged to flourish. What has been said about work and play must be made true for learning. The false dichotomies among this trinity of human activities must be resolved.

Lenin once stated that a measure of civilization was the level of emancipation of women. Canada should become the most civilized country in the world by totally ridding itself of sexism and racism. Every last vestige of sexual separatism should be removed. The principle of diversity coupled to equality should apply legally and operationally to every sex, creed, colour and age. Women, indigenous peoples and other races in Canada are still the victims of laws, attitudes and the practice of exclusion. This leads to diminishment of capacity, the robbery of dignity and other overt and covert forms of discrimination. Anti-nation is a concept in which these false internal divisions, often used for political purposes, are eradicated.

Many years ago the American, Richard Gregg, used the phrase "voluntary simplicity" to describe a life-style of balance between the material and spiritual needs of humans. Gregg's idea incorporates a process of "ephemeralization" whereby we rid ourselves of consumptive excesses and our fixations on property and power. It is not a denial of things, but of thingism; it is not living with deliberate frugality, but making more of less. While voluntary simplicity is guided by the goal of survival, it is no mere surviving, but rather the constant surpassing of oneself in terms of inner growth.

Technology Without Tears
ONE OF THE KEY sub-systems we must restructure in our anti-nation is technology. We must destroy the technological order, that is, the tendency of technology to become autonomous and subvert human will and fulfillment. This does not mean Neo-ludditism, a complete renunciating of science and technology, but it does mean transforming technology to new forms and directing it for human purposes. This author has coined the word "technecology" to embrace the idea of an ecologically sound technology designed for and controlled by people. It would involve minimal material throughput, almost total renewable energy, minimal pollution and maximum recycling, maximum waste utilization and recirculation, labour-intensive and craft-oriented processes and the broad replacement of synthetics by biologicals. All the necessary safeguards prior to use would be observed. Integration with cultural needs,

decentralization, diversity of techniques and smallness of scale would evolve. Agricultural transformations involving organic methods, biological control of pests and the diversity of crops would be developed. The break-down of elitism and profession-alism and the involvement of everybody who is interested in science and technology would be encouraged. The integration of knowledge across all discipline boundaries with no distinction between work and leisure, and the gradual break-down of the sharp distinction between town and country would also evolve. Much of these social and technical changes are yet to be researched and developed but none seems beyond the bounds of realization. Reduction of the scale, imminence and pervasiveness of technology would assist in reducing alienation and elitism. Integration with cultural modes and the development of diversity would have the same effects.

The Institute of Urgent or Relevant Science could have a section dealing entirely with the full development of technology. The ultimate purpose of technology is to restore the human balance with Nature and the necessary balances within Nature, without imposing psychological or physical pain. "Soft" agri-culture must become like husbandry, an enjoyable and esthetic craft. We must also harvest — not hunt — our waters, while conserving their quality. This means investigating the full possibilities of hydroponics and fish farming. Recycling and energy efficiency programs will be key aspects of technology. The intervening development of esthetic and efficient mass transit systems would also be a task for the new technology. The re-design of cities in which recycling was organized much like efficient sewage systems with specific service lines for specific waste materials all directed to a common recycling plant would also be a program for our soft technology. Each city would then be largely independent in its use of recycled paper, metals, fertilizers, etc.

The present tendency for "non-professional" persons to feel alienated by Big Technology and to feel a loss of human sovereignty and autonomy as machines seem to usurp human functions, would have to be stopped and reversed. In part the reversal might be achieved by an education that created bridges rather than gulfs. It might conceivably be assisted by the scaling down of our present large alien technologies. Alienation would certainly be reduced as our technology became subservient to human will and survival.

Before we complete the good news it is most important to reiterate the bad, consisting mainly of the inertia of the present and the momentum of the past. Thus we can identify three dominant collective barriers to the transition to sustainability.

143

These are (1) the existing inventories of attitudes and behaviour of the public; (2) the existing inventory of institutions and their behavioural modes and (3) the existing inventory of hardware. The transitional path must attend to the detailed replacement of these consumption and waste-oriented inventories with conserver-orientations. The limiting barriers tend to be social rather than technical. The rate of replacement is limited by both the physical limits of replacement and the limits on the rates of communication, information and education. A short-cut in the physical realm is retrofit but this in itself has a limiting rate of implementation. Acceleration of all necessary changes can be increased by an all-out massive commitment but this is again limited by a necessary trade-off against the costs of dislocation. We should distribute these distribution costs to the whole of society instead of to the victims of change. We have given information and education high priorities as transitional policies because we believe their realization can be accelerated and also because they are the essential precursor to commitment and involvement. Commitment rapidly follows consensus especially of the "clear and present" danger variety. As a principal, the rate of phasing out and phasing in of the three inventory changes should be equalized to minimize costs of disruption. Through rapid re-distortion of markets and prices, through rapid re-direction of education, through rapid transfer of information and through rapid retrofit of existing physical stock the entire transition cn be accelerated. Crash programs can have net positive effectiveness where consensus exists and costs are equitably shared. "Mutual coercion mutually agreed upon" is a delicate process in any case. The contradictions are powerful. Equity can best be served by government intervention but the cost of equity can be enhanced bureaucracy and decreased incentive. The task of stimulating conservation without sacrificing equity is formidable. Specifically detailing the barriers to a conserver (sustainable society) can aid us in targetting on the necessary changes and assessing resistance to change. Each measure to achieve smooth transition must be matched both to the nature of the targetted goal and the barriers that inhibit its achievement. Both incentive and disincentive must be used appropriately. Such detailed analysis is beyond the scope of ths book but identification of barriers has value in itself. As usual identification of the problems while clearly a prior stage to the search for solution, does not necessarily guarantee that they will be forthcoming.

We should reward conservation and punish waste but within the bounds of "affirmative action", i.e. to protect those who can neither afford higher energy prices or conservation. We should distribute the costs of dislocation suffered by labour and capital for those conservation measures that have social value for all. This is an ethical imperative which the present system has never assumed. Decentralization itself helps to avoid or minimize redistribution costs and unnecessary capital, energy and labour mobility.

Scale, rate and magnitude are all correlated to alienation. In this sense their general reduction humanizes the tools of society.

Job sharing and job trading with shared benefits should be encouraged. Not only does it provide incremental interest through diverse experience but it could serve to extend the number of jobs.

As two broad social and energy principles we should minimize distribution and peaking costs. By providing energy and jobs on-site, i.e. locally and regionally, at an appropriate scale and in an appropriate form we can radically reduce presently high distribution costs while increasing labour and energy stability and reducing costly labour re-distribution impacts. If there are groups of nomadic skilled labourers who prefer mobile, seasonal or cyclical jobs these two can be accomodated through techniques of job sharing and the holding of multiple jobs. A shorter work week and the inclusion of voluntary and other unpaid workers as "gainful" would radically ease unemployment in general. Socially useful should replace gainful in our labour statistics.

There is an intimate and reinforcing mechanism between decentralizing decision-making and human self-realization and self-fulfillment, particularly alienation which derives from a lack of a sense of self-worth and of the capacity for meaningful intervention in one's social and physical environment. People decoupled from grids and meters can become human rather than alienated consumers managing their own homes and lives. People decoupled from the medical bureaucracy can also become more humanized. People managing their own bodes, education and habitats will be essentially less alienated than those who are cogs in the complex dehumanized systems of health, education and energy. One should continue to fear certain negative potentials of pluralism such as the potential loss of life-style, behaviour and attitudinal diversity. The rights of peaceful non-conformity are just as precious in communities of high consensus as in those of low.

In conclusion, the utilities are among the most powerful institutional barriers to conservation. Their permitted liberal debt to equity ratio, their rate structure, their guaranteed return; their peaking problem, their pricing system and the huge social subsidy they receive to encourage supply, all contribute to this. While the large fossil fuel energy exploration, production and distribution corporations in this country have also received huge social subsidies by way of tax credits, ridiculous royalties and generous depletion allowances, attacking the utilities nevertheless offers a larger immediate potential for saving energy. This is not to say that we continue to subsidize fossil fuel producers. Merely by shifting to lower cost co-generation, on-site, district and waste heat generation with its lower capital intensivity, lower distribution costs and its much higher energy efficiency represents a massive saving both in capital and energy. Accompanying this shift at the primary expense of the most costly centralized technology — nuclear, should allow us to have no further nuclear plants in this country at least until the year 2000 and, hopefully, never

It is indeed strange that given the grotesque market and pricing distortions we allow and encourage in the energy supply industries, we are loath to distort the market in favour of renewables. We must demand at least equality of distortion. The double standard of espousing a "free market" to deny the development of renewables while enslaving it to the conventional sources is having it both ways, violating one of our most cherished myths. One of the means of redressing this hypocrisy might be to remandate the utilities to become bankers for conservation in the residential and commercial sector so that their returns are on loans for conservation not on new supply. In general we must wean power away from the ultimate barrier to a sustainable energy policy. This barrier is the political-economy of the industrial-energy complex. Carrots are better than sticks, all else being equal. We can only hope the energy giants' taste for carrots improves rapidly.

The projections of the growth euphorics of today are not unlike those of the anti-growth advocates of the early 1970's. Energy forecasts are incredibly elastic. Growth levels considered essential in 1972 have now been radically cut back but the arguments of growth do not change, just their numbers. This is as true for nuclear power as for total energy forecasts. Official projections of total installed nuclear generating capacity in the year 2000 have been decreasing rapidly since a peak in 1974. In the U.S. the plot of these projections against the year they were made can be soon extrapolated to zero and the Canadian trend is similar. A U.S. Senate report (The Ryan Report) suppressed by the newly formed Department of Energy concludes nuclear power is simply too costly as well as having not merely unresolved but unresolvable problems, i.e. high level waste disposal is not "feasible" and can never be "permanent". Studies on this latter issue by the General Accounting Office (U.S.) and the California Resources and Energy Conservation and Development Commission put to shame our own EMR report and reveal it as whitewash as well as hogwash. Even in Canada it will never wash. The "appointment" of a roving nuclear information commission supposedly neutral is so crude as to have already created a backlash. Public relations has consistently been propaganda on the nuclear issue.

Given these collective barriers to the achievement of anti-nation, the sustainable society, there is nevertheless a strong basis for hope. The human brain with its creative capability, even though it is itself divided between a holistic mode of perception and linear numeracy has evolved as an instrument of survival. Humans are now an endangered species, uniquely so, because of threats of our own making. But the global rise in the consciousness of threat and the commitment to create new societies with high survival value is itself a new exponential. The old order is dying while clinging to its diseases. The new world is coming. No one knows who will win this race but as humans we can only continue to act as if survival can triumph over destruction. There is no need to deny that existential hope is a religion. Faith is a necessary component of change.

Towards a Fourth World: The Empathy State

IT IS MOST appropriate that Paul Sears identified ecology as the "subversive science." This is so because the principles of ecology — indivisibility, inter-relatedness, continuity, harmony, stability and diversity — comprise the web of survival mechanisms which apply not only to plant and animal populations but to human ones as well. It is so because all our systems and social structures violate the ecological imperative.

We have proposed a social model based on ecological principles. Anti-nation is a conceptual model of a multiple but unified nation. Canada as anti-nation would evolve into an ecologically sane society, restructuring its political, economic, technological, social and cultural sub-systems so that they fulfill the ecological imperatives. But more than this, anti-nation is the first stage or launching pad for the ecologizing of life-styles and attitudes, the transformation of material growth goals to the virtually unlimited expansion of human consciousness and creativity and the fusion of individual freedom and community purposes. Incentives, aspirations, and expectations now directed towards acquisition and accumulation of material goods would be transformed toward spiritual goods.

It is no accident that decentralization and a general reduction of scale are intrinsic to survival and based on the capacity to apply ecological principles. Illich calls this the "retooling" of society, or building a "post-industrial tool kit" for survival. The logistics of large urban centres impose the need for "hard" agriculture, excessive food processing, inefficiency in transportation and consumption of energy at very large levels, social and environmental degradation. In effect, such an urban system is "hooked" to perpetuate the increased application of these same processes, which are ultimately suicidal. Each process reinforces the need for the others and we perpetuate the process of degradation. At the same time, the imposition of human monoculture as the form of cultural adaptation destroys diversity and creativity. Again we are drugged into being passive receptors of homogenized cultural goods. The extinction of diversity, combined with over-stimulation, over-crowding, the inhuman scale of technology and huge bureaucracies lead to alienation and a dramatic rise in social pathology of all kinds. Only a drastic reduction of the scale of human settlements, (i.e. de-urbanization and the break-down of the rigid distinction between town and country), the deliberate fostering of diversity of all kinds through decentralization, will enable us to undergo the personal Renaissance we all seek. The recovery of community and the discovery of self rest on applying ecological principles to the means by which we secure food, shelter and clothing, to the processes by which we govern ourselves and our community (not by rule but by release), and to the techniques by which we achieve the capacity for human fulfillment and begin the long journey of psycho-social evolution. There will always be unknowns and always the challenge to know oneself, the other, and the world.

The ecological principles, resting on balance, harmony, mutuality and cooperation, are the only system for the survival of the planet and for resolving the great "Malthusian dilemmas," identified as the Quadrilemma. We require a global budget of resources with limits set by public participation and supported by juridicial standards, not by politicians or technocrats alone. We will then overcome the false dualities of economics and environmental protection, of town and country, of humans and Nature, of community and individual, of challenge and stagnation, of gratification and survival. Only then in that new world, a fourth world, will love replace power as the drive of the human psyche. All our present curves of exponential growth will be transformed from things to human capacities. The syndromes of size and number will be transferred from the material to the spiritual. The "scientific" debates about human nature will move into an entirely new level concerned with the limits — not the depths or confines — that humanity can reach.

It is now clear that the total environment is far broader than the natural environment but includes urban ecology — poverty, over-crowding, noise, stress, social degradation, disorientation and disorganization. We must also extend our concern to all species, to the whole of the biosphere and not to a narrow homocentric view which in itself will be self-defeating because all of life sustains human and all other living things. We agree with John B. Calhoun's concepts of "ideational ecosystem" and "conceptual space," where the principles of ecology also apply. In the same way as we have proposed the need to design the future, we must now plan the evolution of the total environment as part of our revolution. Calhoun has coined the word "$r_x$evolution" as the recipe for the next stage of evolution. The beginning of the next stage he calls "Dawnsday." We can only accuse scientists like Calhoun of being prophets of Dawn.

In terms of involvement we should adopt the existential position that what we do is intrinsically valuable and cannot be measured by any external accounting of success, failure or efficiency. The first step is the ecology of grassroots, the bringing together of all the people comprising the growing consensus in each town, region and country. These people must discover a new politics, become a new constituency and begin the task of identifying goals and priorities which are modest and achievable, and must implement them. Everywhere in the world these movements are beginning to stir.

Thus we have come to conclude that the "necessary revolution" (Ellul) is also the ecological revolution. The present technology and its supportive institutional and bureaucratic forms are anti-ecological. We must "retool" society. This does not mean a new Luddite movement, renouncing technology. It is in fact only with the level of present technical knowledge that we could retool society in a new way.

Finally, we would like to classify this book as a non-academic voyage into a future which secures the future. We have analyzed critical readings of various visionaries. In all these visions the goals of society are either humanely generated or technically imposed. We opt only for the former. The latter rests on the assumption that there is an intrinsic dichotomy between self and society.

The ecological revolution in its ultimate form fuses with Marx's vision of the "withering away of the state" to an anarchic ecologized human community in which the principle is another vision of Marx — "to each according to 'their' needs and from each according to 'their' capacities." But we have not yet witnessed any withering away of states — Marxist or otherwise. In virtually every case, including the possible case of China, the state has become more deeply entrenched in power, bureaucracy

149

and instrument. The excuse is usually the existence of national conflicts involving national securities, always initiated by the "enemy," which leads us back to the need for global solutions.

We have now completed the circle beginning with identification of problems and closing with a vision of a future that is yet to be invented. We have attempted to desribe the path from now to then which leads through abandoning growth, accepting limits and achieving the growth of limits. We cannot pretend that this is other than the greatest challenge ever faced. We will not deny that other voices and other visions may be more appropriate. This book, if anything, is an invitation to a dialogue on the necessary changes and the necessary consensus to make them.

Bibliography

Culture
Bateson, Gregory, *Towards an Ecology of Mind*, Ballantine, New York, 1973. Beauvoir, Simone de, *The Second Sex*, Penguin, Harmondsworth, Middlesex, 1972. Fromm, Erich, *Man for Himself*, Routledge and Kegan, Paul, London, 1971. Fromm, Erich, *The Sane Society*, Routledge and Kegan, Paul, London, 1956. Goodman, Paul, *Growing Up Absurd*, Gollancz, V., London, 1961. Henderson, Hazel, *Creating Alternative Futures*, Berkely Publishing, New York, 1978. Laing, R.D., *The Divided Self*, Pelican Books, London, 1965. Laing, R.D., *The Politics of Experience*, Pelican Books, 1967. Marcuse, Herbert, *One Dimensional Man*, Sphere Books, 1968. Mead, Margaret, *Cultural Patterns and Technical Change*, Lectures for the American Museum of Natural History, 1955. Maslow, Abraham, *Motivation and Personality*, Harper & Row, New York, 1954. McLuhan, Marshall, *Understanding Media*, Routledge and Kegan, Paul, London, 1964. Nickerson, Mike, *Bakavi*, All About Us—Nous Autres Inc., Ottawa, 1977. Robertson, James, *The Sane Alternative*, Villiers, London, 1978. Roszak, Theodore, *The Making of a Counter Culture*, Faber and Faber, London, 1970. Slater, Philip, *The Pursuit of Loneliness*, Beacon Press, Boston, 1970. Taylor, Gordon Rattray, *Rethink: A Paraprimitive Solution*, Chaucer Press, Bungey, Suffolk, 1972. Wallace, Anthony, *Culture and Personality*, Random Press, New York, 1963.

Economics
Boulding, K.E., "The Economics of the Coming Spaceship Earth" in *Environmental Quality In a Growing Economy* (Ed. Jarrete), Johns Hopkins Press, Resources for the Future, 1976. Daly,

Herman E., ed. *Towards a Steady State Economy*, W.H. Freeman, San Francisco, 1973. Galbraith, J.K., *The New Industrial State*, Pelican Books, 1974. Georgescu-Roegen, N., *The Entropy Law and the Economic Process*, Harvard University Press, Cambridge, 1971. Henderson, Hazel, "A Farewell to the Corporate State", *Business & Society Review*, Spring, 1976; see also "Creating Alternative Futures" (Culture). Henderson, Hazel, "The Entropy State", *Planning Review*, April/May, 1974. Polanyi, Karl, *Primitive, Archaic and Modern Economics*, Doubleday, New York, 1968. Mishan, E.J., *The Costs of Economic Growth*, Staples Press, London, 1967. Mishan, E.J., *The Economic Growth Debate*, Allen and Unwin, London, 1977. Robertson, James, *Power, Money and Sex*, Marion Boyars Publishers Ltd., London, 1976. Schumacher, E.F., *Small is Beautiful*, Sphere Books, London, 1973.

Energy
Commoner, Barry, *The Poverty of Power*, Alfred A. Knopf, New York, 1976. Crane, David, "Canada's Energy Crisis", *Toronto Star*, October 11, 15, 16, 17, 1973. Dumas, Lloyd J., *The Conservation Response*, Lexington Books, Lexington, Mass., 1976. "Jobs and Energy", *Environmentalists for Full Employment*, Washington, D.C., Spring, 1977. Freeman, David, *A Time to Choose* (Report of the Ford Foundation Energy Policy), Ballinger Publishing Co., Cambridge, Mass., 1974. "Energy Scenarios for New Zealand", Harris, G.S. et al., N.Z., E.R. & D. Committee Report #19, March, 1977. "Energy Scenarios for the Future", Hedlin, Menzies & Associates Ltd., Science Council of Canada, July, 1976. Herman, S.W. and Malefatto, A.J., *Energy Futures: Industry and New Technologies*, Ballinger Publishing Company, Cambridge, Mass., 1977. Illich, Ivan D., *Energy and Equity*, Calder and Boyars and Company, Garden City, N.Y., 1974. Lovins, A.B., *World Energy Strategies*, Ballinger Publishing Co., Cambridge, Mass., 1975. Lovins, A.B., *Soft Energy Paths: Towards a Durable Peace*, Ballinger Publishing Company, Cambridge, Mass., 1977. McCallum, Bruce, "Environmentally Appropriate Technology", Environment Canada, Ottawa, 1975. Odum, Herbert T., *Environment, Power and Society*, Wiley Interscience, N.Y., 1972. Price, J.H., *Dynamic Energy Analysis and Nuclear Power*, Friends of the Earth, London, 1974. Ross, Marc M., and Williams, R., "The Potential for Fuel Conservation", *Technology Review*, pp. 49-57, February, 1977. "Conserver Society Notes", Science Council of Canada, Vol. 1, Nos. 1 to 4, Vol. 2, Nos. 1 & 2. Schipper, Les and Lichtenberg, Allan J., "Efficient Energy Use and Well-Being: The Swedish Example", *Science* 194, pp. 1001-1013, 3 Dec. 1976. Schurr, Sam H., (ed.) *Energy, Economic Growth and the Environment*, Resources for the Future, Johns Hopkins

University Press, 1972.

Environment
Commoner, Barry, *The Closing Circle*, Bantam, New York, 1971. Carson, Rachel, *Silent Spring*, Fawcett, Greenwich, Conn., 1962. Dansereau, Pierre, "Harmony and Discord in the Canadian Environment", Canadian Envrionmental Advisory Council, Occasional Paper No. 1, Publications Distribution Centre, Environment Canada, Ottawa, Canada. Ehrlich, Paul, *The End of Affluence*, Ballantyne Books, New York, 1974. Hardin, Garrett, "The Tragedy of the Commons", *Science* 162, pp. 1243-1248, 13 Dec. 1968. Leopold, Aldo, *A Sand County Almanac*, Oxford University Press, New York, 1966. Odum, Eugene P., *Fundamentals of Ecology*, W.B. Saunders Company, Toronto, 1971. Owen, Oliver S., *Natural Resource Conservation*, Macmillan, New York, 1971. Shepherd, Paul and McKinley, Daniel, eds., *The Subversive Science*, Houghton, Miflin, Boston, 1969.

General
Adams, Ian, *The Real Poverty Report*, M.G. Hurtig Ltd., Edmonton, 1971. Barnes, Barry, ed., *Sociology of Science*, Penguin Books, Harmoundsworth, Middlesex, 1973. Beer, Stafford, *Designing Freedom*, John Wiley and Sons, New York, 1975. Bell, Daniel, *Toward the Year 2000*, Houghton, Mifflin, New York, 1968. Cardinal, Harold, *The Unjust Society*, Hurtig Publishers, Edmonton, 1973. Chardin, Teilhard de, *The Future of Man*, Harper and Row, New York, 1959. Dosman, E.J., *The National Interest*, McLennad and Stewart, Toronto, 1975. Ehrlich, Paul, *The End of Affluence*, Ballantyne Books, New York, 1974. Ellul, Jacques, *The Autopsy of Revolution*, translated from French by Patrica West (1st American edition) Knopf, New York, 1971. Ellul, Jacques, *The Technological Society*, Jonathan Cape, London, 1965. Freeman, David, *Technology and Society*, Rand, McNally, Chicago, 1974. Hardin, Garrett, "The Tragedy of the Commons" (see Environment). Goldsmith, Edward, ed., *Can Britain Survive?* Sphere Books, London, 1971. Hurtig, M.G., "Canada's Resources: Independence and Responsibility" prepared for Centre for Advanced Concepts, Environment Canada, 1974. Henderson, Hazel, "Ideologies, Paradigms and Myths: Changes in our Operative Social Values", *Liberal Education*, May, 1976. Illich, Harold A., *A Celebration of Awareness*, University of Toronto Press, Toronto, 1972. Jones, Charles O., *An Introduction to the Study of Public Policy*, Wadsworth, Belmont, Calif., 1970. Kuhn, Thomas, *The Structure of Scientific Revolutions*, University of Chicago Press, Chicago, 1962. Mead, Margaret, *Cultural Patterns and Technical Change*, (see Culture). Meadows, D. et al., *The*

Limits to Growth, New American Library, New York, 1972; also editor *Alternatives to Growth*, Ballinger, Cambridge, Mass., 1977. Merton, Robert K., *Social Theory and Social Structure*, The Free Press, New York, 1967. Mesarovic, M. and Pestal, E., *Mankind at the Turning Point*, Dutton, New York, 1974. Mumford, Lewis, *Technics and Civilization*, Harcourt Brace and World Inc., New York, 1962. Nickerson, Mike, "Bakavi", (see Culture). Pirages, Dennis Clark, *The Sustainable Society*, Praeger Publishers, New York, 1977. Polanyi, Karl, *Primitive, Archaic and Modern Economics* (see Economics). Primack, J. and Von Hippel, F., *Advice and Dissent*, Basic Books Inc., New York, 1976. Renshaw, Edward, *The End of Progress*, Duxbury Press, North Scituate, Mass., 1976. Robertson, James, *Power, Money and Sex*, (see Economics). Schon, Donald, *Beyond the Stable State*, Temple Smith, London, 1971. Toffler, Alvin, *Future Shock*, Random House, New York, 1970. Tinbergen, Jan, *RIO-Reshaping the International Order*, New American Library, New York, 1976. Schumacher, E.F., *Small is Beautiful*, (see Economics). Science Council of Canada, "Conserver Society Notes", (see Energy). Warner, J.W. *Partner to Behemoth*, New Press, Toronto, 1970. Winthrop, Henry, *Ventures in Social Interpretation*, Appleton-Century-Crofts, New York, 1968.

Nuclear
Barber, R.J. and Associates, "LDC Nuclear Power Projects 1975-1980", ERDA No. 52, Washington, 1975. "Fact Finding Group on Nuclear Power", The Burns Report, New Zealand, 1977. "Nuclear Power and the Environment", The Flowers Commission, London HMSO, Sept., 1976. "Impact of a 30 year Nuclear Moratorium on the U.S." (1985-2015), Institute of Energy Policy Analysis, Oak Ridge Associated Universities, Oak Ridge, Tenn., 1976. "Nuclear Power: Issues and Choices", Mitre Corporation sponsored by the Ford Foundation, Ballinger Publishing, Cambridge, Mass., 1977. "Ranger Uranium Environmental Enquiry", The Fox Reports I and II, Australian Government Publishing Service, Canberra, 1976. Kendall, Henry W. et al, "The Nuclear Fuel Cycle", The Union of Concerned Scientists, Boston, Mass., 1974. Knelman, F.H. *Nuclear Energy: The Unforgiving Technology*, Hurtig Publishers, Edmonton, 1976. Lovins, A.B. *Non-Nuclear Futures*, Ballinger Publishing, Cambridge, Mass., 1975. Patterson, Walter C., *Nuclear Power*, Penguin, Harmoundsworth, Middlesex, 1967. Price, J.H. *Dynamic Energy Analysis and Nuclear Power*, (see Energy)

Population
Ehrlich, Anne H., and Ehrlich, Paul, *Resources Environment and*

Population, W.H. Freeman, San Francisco, 1970. Ehrlich, Paul, *The Population Bomb*, Sierra-Ballantyne, New York, 1968. Marsden, Lorna, ed., *Population Probe: Canada*, Copp Clark, Toronto, 1972. "Perceptions" Nos. 1 and 4, Science Council of Canada, Population, Urbanization and Food, 1976.

Technology
Allen, Francis R., et al., *Technology and Social Change*, Appleton-Century-Crofts, New York, 1957. Commoner, Barry, *The Closing Circle*, Bantam, New York, 1971. Ellul, Jacques, *The Technological Society*, (see General). Grant, George, *Technology and Empire*, House of Anansi, Toronto, 1967. Haddon, William Jr., "On the Escape of Tigers: An Ecologic Note", *Technology Review*, May, 1970. Illich, Ivan D., *Tools for Conviviality*, Harper and Row, New York, 1973. Knelman, F.H., *1984 and All That*, Wadsworth, Belmont, Calif., 1970. McCallum, Bruce, *Environmentally Appropriate Technology*, (see Energy). Mumford, Lewis, *Technics and Civilization*, (see General). Price, Derek J. de Solla, *Little Science, Big Science*, Columbia University Press, New York, 1963. Price, D.K., *Government and Science*, Oxford University Press, 1962. Primack, J. and Von Hippel, T., *Advice and Dissent*, (see General). Roszak, Theodore, *The Making of a Counter Culture*, (see Culture). Sklair, Leslie, *Organized Knowledge*, Paladin, London, 1973. Stover, Carl F., *The Technological Order*, Wayne State University Press, Detroit, 1963. Weinberg, Alvin, *Reflections on Big Science*, M.I.T. Press, Boston, 1967.

Urbanization
Detwyler, Thomas R. et al., *Urbanization and Environment*, Wadsworth, Belmont, Calif., 1972. Krueger, Ralph R., and Bryfogle, Charles, eds., *Urban Problems: A Canadian Reader*, Holt, Rinehart and Winston, Montreal, 1971. Mumford, Lewis, *The City in History*, Penguin, Harmoundsworth, Middlesex, 1961. Mumford, Lewis, *The Urban Prospect*, Harcourt, Brace and World Inc., New York, 1968. Science Council of Canada, "Perceptions", (see Population). Ward, Barbara, "Human Settlements: Crisis and Opportunity", Information Canada, Ottawa, 1974.